THE WTO
DISPUTE SETTLEMENT
PROCEDURES

A Collection of the Legal Texts

World Trade Organization
Geneva, August 1995

PREFACE

This volume contains a collection of the legal texts related to the settlement of disputes under the GATT 1947 and the Agreement Establishing the World Trade Organization (WTO). To facilitate their use the texts have been grouped by subject matter, and brief notes in the margin, cross-references and a subject index have been added by the WTO Secretariat. These additions do not form part of the legal texts and therefore should not be used as sources of interpretation.

This publication was prepared by Gabrielle Marceau and Peter Morrison.

A repertoire of the dispute settlement practice under the GATT 1947 can be found in the *"Analytical Index: Guide to GATT Law and Practice"* published by the WTO Secretariat.

Frieder Roessler
Director
Legal Affairs Division
World Trade Organization
August 1995

ABBREVIATIONS

In this publication, the following abbreviations have been used:

ADP	Agreement on Implementation of Article VI of GATT 1994;
Aircraft	Tokyo Round Agreement on Trade in Civil Aircraft;
BISD	Basic Instruments and Selected Documents (published by GATT);
CPs	CONTRACTING PARTIES;
CTG	Council for Trade in Goods;
CTS	Council for Trade in Services;
Customs Valuation	Agreement on Implementation of Article VII of GATT 1994;
Dairy	International Dairy Agreement;
DSB	Dispute Settlement Body;
DSU	Understanding on Rules and Procedures Governing the Settlement of Disputes;
GATS	General Agreement on Trade in Services;
GPA	Agreement on Government Procurement;
Montreal Decision	Decision of 12 April 1989 on dispute settlement (BISD 36S/61) adopted by the CPs following the Mid-Term Review of the Uruguay Round Negotiations;
PGE	Permanent Group of Experts;
SCM	Agreement on Subsidies and Countervailing Measures;
SPS	Agreement on the Application of Sanitary and Phytosanitary Measures;
TBT	Agreement on Technical Barriers to Trade;
Textile	Agreement on Textiles and Clothing;
TMB	Textiles Monitoring Body;
Transitional Arrangements	Decisions adopted on 8 December 1994 to facilitate the transition from the GATT to the WTO;
1966 Decision	Decision of 5 April 1966 on Procedures under (GATT) Article XXIII (BISD 14S/18).

TABLE OF CONTENTS

INDEX

ARBITRATION

ASSISTANCE, legal and technical

BENEFITS (impairment of)

CLAIMS

COMPENSATION (and suspension of concessions)

CONCILIATION

CONFIDENTIALITY

CONFIDENTIALITY

CONFLICT OF LAWS

CONSENSUS

CONSULTATIONS

DEVELOPING COUNTRY

DISPUTE SETTLEMENT BODY (DSB)

ENFORCEMENT

> See IMPLEMENTATION, COMPENSATION and
> SUSPENSION OF CONCESSIONS

EVIDENCE

EXPERTS

FINDINGS

GOOD OFFICES, CONCILIATION AND MEDIATION

IMPLEMENTATION

see also COMPENSATION and SUSPENSION
OF CONCESSIONS

INDICATIVE LIST (panelists)

INFORMATION

INTERIM REVIEW

INTERPRETATION

JURISDICTION

NULLIFICATION OR IMPAIRMENT

PANEL

PANEL (cont.)

PERMANENT GROUP OF EXPERTS

PROCEDURE

REASONABLE PERIOD OF TIME (implementation)

RECOMMENDATIONS AND OR RULINGS

TRANSITION

TRANSPARENCY

URGENCY

UNDERSTANDING ON RULES AND PROCEDURES GOVERNING THE SETTLEMENT OF DISPUTES*

Members hereby *agree* as follows:

Article 1

Coverage and Application

1.   The rules and procedures of this Understanding shall apply to disputes brought pursuant to the consultation and dispute settlement provisions of the agreements listed in Appendix 1 to this Understanding (referred to in this Understanding as the "covered agreements"). The rules and procedures of this Understanding shall also apply to consultations and the settlement of disputes between Members concerning their rights and obligations under the provisions of the Agreement Establishing the World Trade Organization (referred to in this Understanding as the "WTO Agreement") and of this Understanding taken in isolation or in combination with any other covered agreement. *agreements covered*

2.   The rules and procedures of this Understanding shall apply subject to such special or additional rules and procedures on dispute settlement contained in the covered agreements as are identified in Appendix 2 to this Understanding. To the extent that there is a difference between the rules and procedures of this Understanding and the special or additional rules and procedures set forth in Appendix 2, the special or additional rules and procedures in Appendix 2 shall prevail. In disputes involving rules and procedures under more than one covered agreement, if there is a conflict between special or additional rules and procedures of such agreements under review, and where the parties to the dispute cannot agree on rules and procedures within 20 days of the establishment of the panel, the Chairman of the Dispute Settlement Body provided for in paragraph 1 of Article 2 (referred to in this Understanding as the "DSB"), in consultation with the parties *special or additional rules*   *conflict*

*   Annex 2 of the Marrakesh Agreement Establishing the World Trade Organization. This Agreement is hereinafter referred to as the WTO Agreement.

to the dispute, shall determine the rules and procedures to be followed within 10 days after a request by either Member. The Chairman shall be guided by the principle that special or additional rules and procedures should be used where possible, and the rules and procedures set out in this Understanding should be used to the extent necessary to avoid conflict.

Article 2

Administration

competence of DSB

1.   The Dispute Settlement Body is hereby established to administer these rules and procedures and, except as otherwise provided in a covered agreement, the consultation and dispute settlement provisions of the covered agreements. Accordingly, the DSB shall have the authority to establish panels, adopt panel and Appellate Body reports, maintain surveillance of implementation of rulings and recommendations, and authorize suspension of concessions and other obligations under the covered agreements. With respect to disputes arising under a covered agreement which is a Plurilateral Trade Agreement, the term "Member" as

special composition

used herein shall refer only to those Members that are parties to the relevant Plurilateral Trade Agreement. Where the DSB administers the dispute settlement provisions of a Plurilateral Trade Agreement, only those Members that are parties to that Agreement may participate in decisions or actions taken by the DSB with respect to that dispute.

duty to inform other WTO bodies

2.   The DSB shall inform the relevant WTO Councils and Committees of any developments in disputes related to provisions of the respective covered agreements.

meetings

3.   The DSB shall meet as often as necessary to carry out its functions within the time-frames provided in this Understanding.

decision making

4.   Where the rules and procedures of this Understanding provide for the DSB to take a decision, it shall do so by consensus.[1]

---

[1]   The DSB shall be deemed to have decided by consensus on a matter submitted for its consideration, if no Member, present at the meeting of the DSB when the decision is taken, formally objects to the proposed decision.

Article 3

General Provisions

1. Members affirm their adherence to the principles for the management of disputes heretofore applied under Articles XXII and XXIII of GATT 1947, and the rules and procedures as further elaborated and modified herein.

prior practice

2. The dispute settlement system of the WTO is a central element in providing security and predictability to the multilateral trading system. The Members recognize that it serves to preserve the rights and obligations of Members under the covered agreements, and to clarify the existing provisions of those agreements in accordance with customary rules of interpretation of public international law. Recommendations and rulings of the DSB cannot add to or diminish the rights and obligations provided in the covered agreements.

functions of dispute settlement system

3. The prompt settlement of situations in which a Member considers that any benefits accruing to it directly or indirectly under the covered agreements are being impaired by measures taken by another Member is essential to the effective functioning of the WTO and the maintenance of a proper balance between the rights and obligations of Members.

prompt settlement

4. Recommendations or rulings made by the DSB shall be aimed at achieving a satisfactory settlement of the matter in accordance with the rights and obligations under this Understanding and under the covered agreements.

aim of recommendations or rulings

5. All solutions to matters formally raised under the consultation and dispute settlement provisions of the covered agreements, including arbitration awards, shall be consistent with those agreements and shall not nullify or impair benefits accruing to any Member under those agreements, nor impede the attainment of any objective of those agreements.

consistency of solutions with covered agreements

6. Mutually agreed solutions to matters formally raised under the consultation and dispute settlement provisions of the covered agreements shall be notified to the DSB and the relevant Councils and Committees, where any Member may raise any point relating thereto.

mutually agreed solutions

7. Before bringing a case, a Member shall exercise its judgement as to whether action under these procedures would be fruitful. The aim of the dispute settlement mechanism is to secure

aim of dispute settlement mechanism

withdrawal
of inconsistent
measures

compensation

a positive solution to a dispute. A solution mutually acceptable to the parties to a dispute and consistent with the covered agreements is clearly to be preferred. In the absence of a mutually agreed solution, the first objective of the dispute settlement mechanism is usually to secure the withdrawal of the measures concerned if these are found to be inconsistent with the provisions of any of the covered agreements. The provision of compensation should be resorted to only if the immediate withdrawal of the measure is impracticable and as a temporary measure pending the withdrawal of the measure which is inconsistent with a covered agreement. The last resort which this Understanding provides to the Member invoking the dispute settlement procedures is the possibility of suspending the application of concessions or other obligations under the covered agreements on a discriminatory basis vis-à-vis the other Member, subject to authorization by the DSB of such measures.

retaliation

presumption
of nullification
or impairment

8.   In cases where there is an infringement of the obligations assumed under a covered agreement, the action is considered *prima facie* to constitute a case of nullification or impairment. This means that there is normally a presumption that a breach of the rules has an adverse impact on other Members parties to that covered agreement, and in such cases, it shall be up to the Member against whom the complaint has been brought to rebut the charge.

authoritative
interpretations

9.   The provisions of this Understanding are without prejudice to the rights of Members to seek authoritative interpretation of provisions of a covered agreement through decision-making under the WTO Agreement or a covered agreement which is a Plurilateral Trade Agreement.

good faith

10.   It is understood that requests for conciliation and the use of the dispute settlement procedures should not be intended or considered as contentious acts and that, if a dispute arises, all Members will engage in these procedures in good faith in an effort to resolve the dispute. It is also understood that complaints and counter-complaints in regard to distinct matters should not be linked.

complaints and
counter-complaints

transitional rules

11.   This Understanding shall be applied only with respect to new requests for consultations under the consultation provisions of the covered agreements made on or after the date of entry into force of the WTO Agreement. With respect to disputes for which the request for consultations was made under GATT 1947 or

under any other predecessor agreement to the covered agreements before the date of entry into force of the WTO Agreement, the relevant dispute settlement rules and procedures in effect immediately prior to the date of entry into force of the WTO Agreement shall continue to apply.[2]

See also Decisions on Transitional Arrangements at p. 78 .

12. Notwithstanding paragraph 11, if a complaint based on any of the covered agreements is brought by a developing country Member against a developed country Member, the complaining party shall have the right to invoke, as an alternative to the provisions contained in Articles 4, 5, 6 and 12 of this Understanding, the corresponding provisions of the Decision of 5 April 1966 (BISD 14S/18), except that where the Panel considers that the time-frame provided for in paragraph 7 of that Decision is insufficient to provide its report and with the agreement of the complaining party, that time-frame may be extended. To the extent that there is a difference between the rules and procedures of Articles 4, 5, 6 and 12 and the corresponding rules and procedures of the Decision, the latter shall prevail.

developing country

See also the 1966 Decision at p. 75 .

Article 4

Consultations

1. Members affirm their resolve to strengthen and improve the effectiveness of the consultation procedures employed by Members.

effectiveness

2. Each Member undertakes to accord sympathetic consideration to and afford adequate opportunity for consultation regarding any representations made by another Member concerning measures affecting the operation of any covered agreement taken within the territory of the former.[3]

sympathetic consideration

3. If a request for consultations is made pursuant to a covered agreement, the Member to which the request is made shall, unless otherwise mutually agreed, reply to the request within 10 days after the date of its receipt and shall enter into consultations in good

time period

---

[2]   This paragraph shall also be applied to disputes on which panel reports have not been adopted or fully implemented.

[3]   Where the provisions of any other covered agreement concerning measures taken by regional or local governments or authorities within the territory of a Member contain provisions different from the provisions of this paragraph, the provisions of such other covered agreement shall prevail.

faith within a period of no more than 30 days after the date of receipt of the request, with a view to reaching a mutually satisfactory solution. If the Member does not respond within 10 days after the date of receipt of the request, or does not enter into consultations within a period of no more than 30 days, or a period otherwise mutually agreed, after the date of receipt of the request, then the Member that requested the holding of consultations may proceed directly to request the establishment of a panel.

notification to WTO bodies

4.   All such requests for consultations shall be notified to the DSB and the relevant Councils and Committees by the Member which requests consultations. Any request for consultations shall be submitted in writing and shall give the reasons for the request, including identification of the measures at issue and an indication of the legal basis for the complaint.

> *See GATT 1994 XXII:1 and XXIII:1 at p. 43; SCM 4.2, 4.3 at p. 60, 7 at p. 62; GATS XXII at p. 68; TRIPS 64 at p. 72; GPA XXII:1, 2 at p. 92; Aircraft 8.5, 8.6 at p. 95; Dairy IV:5 at p. 97, as well as provisions on consultations contained in other WTO covered agreements at p. 38.*

attempt to obtain settlement

5.   In the course of consultations in accordance with the provisions of a covered agreement, before resorting to further action under this Understanding, Members should attempt to obtain satisfactory adjustment of the matter.

confidential, without prejudice

6.   Consultations shall be confidential, and without prejudice to the rights of any Member in any further proceedings.

time period for request for panel

7.   If the consultations fail to settle a dispute within 60 days after the date of receipt of the request for consultations, the complaining party may request the establishment of a panel. The complaining party may request a panel during the 60-day period if the consulting parties jointly consider that consultations have failed to settle the dispute.

> *See DSU 12.10 for developing country.*

cases of urgency

8.   In cases of urgency, including those which concern perishable goods, Members shall enter into consultations within a period of no more than 10 days after the date of receipt of the request. If the consultations have failed to settle the dispute within a period of 20 days after the date of receipt of the request, the complaining party may request the establishment of a panel.

9.   In cases of urgency, including those which concern perishable goods, the parties to the dispute, panels and the Appellate

Body shall make every effort to accelerate the proceedings to the greatest extent possible.

10.   During consultations Members should give special atten- *developing*
tion to the particular problems and interests of developing country *countries*
Members.

11.   Whenever a Member other than the consulting Members *joint consultations*
considers that it has a substantial trade interest in consultations
being held pursuant to paragraph 1 of Article XXII of GATT
1994, paragraph 1 of Article XXII of GATS, or the corresponding
provisions in other covered agreements[4], such Member may
notify the consulting Members and the DSB, within 10 days after
the date of the circulation of the request for consultations under
said Article, of its desire to be joined in the consultations. Such
Member shall be joined in the consultations, provided that the
Member to which the request for consultations was addressed
agrees that the claim of substantial interest is well-founded. In that
event they shall so inform the DSB. If the request to be joined in
the consultations is not accepted, the applicant Member shall be
free to request consultations under paragraph 1 of Article XXII or
paragraph 1 of Article XXIII of GATT 1994, paragraph 1 of
Article XXII or paragraph 1 of Article XXIII of GATS, or the
corresponding provisions in other covered agreements.

See at p. 38 the provisions referred to in footnote 4 below.

Article 5

Good Offices, Conciliation and Mediation

1.   Good offices, conciliation and mediation are procedures *voluntary*
that are undertaken voluntarily if the parties to the dispute so
agree.

---

[4]   The corresponding consultation provisions in the covered agreements are listed
hereunder: Agreement on Agriculture, Article 19; Agreement on the Application of
Sanitary and Phytosanitary Measures, paragraph 1 of Article 11; Agreement on Textiles
and Clothing, paragraph 4 of Article 8; Agreement on Technical Barriers to Trade,
paragraph 1 of Article 14; Agreement on Trade-Related Investment Measures, Article
8; Agreement on Implementation of Article VI of GATT 1994, paragraph 2 of Article
17; Agreement on Implementation of Article VII of GATT 1994, paragraph 2 of Article
19; Agreement on Preshipment Inspection, Article 7; Agreement on Rules of Origin,
Article 7; Agreement on Import Licensing Procedures, Article 6; Agreement on
Subsidies and Countervailing Measures, Article 30; Agreement on Safeguards, Article
14; Agreement on Trade-Related Aspects of Intellectual Property Rights, Article 64.1;
and any corresponding consultation provisions in Plurilateral Trade Agreements as
determined by the competent bodies of each Agreement and as notified to the DSB.

confidential

2.　　Proceedings involving good offices, conciliation and mediation, and in particular positions taken by the parties to the dispute during these proceedings, shall be confidential, and with-

without prejudice

out prejudice to the rights of either party in any further proceedings under these procedures.

initiation

3.　　Good offices, conciliation or mediation may be requested at any time by any party to a dispute. They may begin at any time and

termination

be terminated at any time. Once procedures for good offices, conciliation or mediation are terminated, a complaining party may then proceed with a request for the establishment of a panel.

time periods

4.　　When good offices, conciliation or mediation are entered into within 60 days after the date of receipt of a request for consultations, the complaining party must allow a period of 60 days after the date of receipt of the request for consultations before

request for panel

requesting the establishment of a panel. The complaining party may request the establishment of a panel during the 60-day period if the parties to the dispute jointly consider that the good offices, conciliation or mediation process has failed to settle the dispute.

concurrent panel proceedings

5.　　If the parties to a dispute agree, procedures for good offices, conciliation or mediation may continue while the panel process proceeds.

Director-General

6.　　The Director-General may, acting in an *ex officio* capacity, offer good offices, conciliation or mediation with the view to assisting Members to settle a dispute.

Article 6

Establishment of Panels

time period for establishment

1.　　If the complaining party so requests, a panel shall be established at the latest at the DSB meeting following that at which the request first appears as an item on the DSB's agenda, unless at that meeting the DSB decides by consensus not to establish a panel.[5]

See also ADP 17.5 at p. 54; SCM 4.4, 7.4 at pp. 59 and 61; GPA XXII:3 at p. 91.

request for establishment

2.　　The request for the establishment of a panel shall be made in writing. It shall indicate whether consultations were held, identify the

---

[5]　　If the complaining party so requests, a meeting of the DSB shall be convened for this purpose within 15 days of the request, provided that at least 10 days' advance notice of the meeting is given.

specific measures at issue and provide a brief summary of the legal basis of the complaint sufficient to present the problem clearly. In case the applicant requests the establishment of a panel with other than standard terms of reference, the written request shall include the proposed text of special terms of reference.

Article 7

Terms of Reference of Panels

1. Panels shall have the following terms of reference unless the parties to the dispute agree otherwise within 20 days from the establishment of the panel:

standard terms of reference

> "To examine, in the light of the relevant provisions in (name of the covered agreement(s) cited by the parties to the dispute), the matter referred to the DSB by (name of party) in document ... and to make such findings as will assist the DSB in making the recommendations or in giving the rulings provided for in that/those agreement(s)."

2. Panels shall address the relevant provisions in any covered agreement or agreements cited by the parties to the dispute.

mandate of panel

3. In establishing a panel, the DSB may authorize its Chairman to draw up the terms of reference of the panel in consultation with the parties to the dispute, subject to the provisions of paragraph 1. The terms of reference thus drawn up shall be circulated to all Members. If other than standard terms of reference are agreed upon, any Member may raise any point relating thereto in the DSB.

other than standard terms of reference

See also DSU Appdx 4.1 at p. 36; GPA XXII:4 at p. 91.

Article 8

Composition of Panels

1. Panels shall be composed of well-qualified governmental and/or non-governmental individuals, including persons who have served on or presented a case to a panel, served as a representative of a Member or of a contracting party to GATT 1947 or as a representative to the Council or Committee of any covered agreement or its predecessor agreement, or in the Secretariat, taught or published on international trade law or policy, or served as a senior trade policy official of a Member.

qualifications of panelists

See also GATS, Annex on Financial Services Art. 4 at p. 70 and GATS, Decision on Certain Dispute Settlement Procedures Art. 3 and 4 at p. 71; GPA XXII:5 at p. 91.

2.   Panel members should be selected with a view to ensuring the independence of the members, a sufficiently diverse background and a wide spectrum of experience.

3.   Citizens of Members whose governments[6] are parties to the dispute or third parties as defined in paragraph 2 of Article 10 shall not serve on a panel concerned with that dispute, unless the parties to the dispute agree otherwise.

indicative list of panelists

4.   To assist in the selection of panelists, the Secretariat shall maintain an indicative list of governmental and non-governmental individuals possessing the qualifications outlined in paragraph 1, from which panelists may be drawn as appropriate. That list shall include the roster of non-governmental panelists established on 30 November 1984 (BISD 31S/9), and other rosters and indicative lists established under any of the covered agreements, and shall retain the names of persons on those rosters and indicative lists at the time of entry into force of the WTO Agreement. Members may periodically suggest names of governmental and non-governmental individuals for inclusion on the indicative list, providing relevant information on their knowledge of international trade and of the sectors or subject matter of the covered agreements, and those names shall be added to the list upon approval by the DSB. For each of the individuals on the list, the list shall indicate specific areas of experience or expertise of the individuals in the sectors or subject matter of the covered agreements.

See Decision on Certain Dispute Settlement Procedures for the GATS Art. 5 at p. 71.

size of panel, notification of composition

5.   Panels shall be composed of three panelists unless the parties to the dispute agree, within 10 days from the establishment of the panel, to a panel composed of five panelists. Members shall be informed promptly of the composition of the panel.

---

6   In the case where customs unions or common markets are parties to a dispute, this provision applies to citizens of all member countries of the customs unions or common markets.

6.   The Secretariat shall propose nominations for the panel to *nomination* the parties to the dispute. The parties to the dispute shall not oppose *of panelists* nominations except for compelling reasons.

7.   If there is no agreement on the panelists within 20 days after *determination of* the date of the establishment of a panel, at the request of either *composition by the* party, the Director-General, in consultation with the Chairman of *Director-General* the DSB and the Chairman of the relevant Council or Committee, shall determine the composition of the panel by appointing the panelists whom the Director-General considers most appropriate in accordance with any relevant special or additional rules or procedures of the covered agreement or covered agreements which are at issue in the dispute, after consulting with the parties to the dispute. The Chairman of the DSB shall inform the Members of the composition of the panel thus formed no later than 10 days after the date the Chairman receives such a request.

8.   Members shall undertake, as a general rule, to permit their *permission to serve* officials to serve as panelists.

9.   Panelists shall serve in their individual capacities and not as *impartiality* government representatives, nor as representatives of any organiza- *of panelists* tion. Members shall therefore not give them instructions nor seek to influence them as individuals with regard to matters before a panel.

10.   When a dispute is between a developing country Member *composition in* and a developed country Member the panel shall, if the developing *cases involving a* country Member so requests, include at least one panelist from a *developing country* developing country Member.

11.   Panelists' expenses, including travel and subsistence allow- *expenses* ance, shall be met from the WTO budget in accordance with criteria to be adopted by the General Council, based on recommendations of the Committee on Budget, Finance and Administration.

Article 9
Procedures for Multiple Complainants

1.   Where more than one Member requests the establishment of *single panel* a panel related to the same matter, a single panel may be estab- *to examine* lished to examine these complaints taking into account the rights of all Members concerned. A single panel should be established to examine such complaints whenever feasible.

2.   The single panel shall organize its examination and present *rights maintained* its findings to the DSB in such a manner that the rights which the

parties to the dispute would have enjoyed had separate panels examined the complaints are in no way impaired. If one of the parties to the dispute so requests, the panel shall submit separate reports on the dispute concerned. The written submissions by each of the complainants shall be made available to the other complainants, and each complainant shall have the right to be present when any one of the other complainants presents its views to the panel.

multiple panels

3.   If more than one panel is established to examine the complaints related to the same matter, to the greatest extent possible the same persons shall serve as panelists on each of the separate panels and the timetable for the panel process in such disputes shall be harmonized.

Article 10
Third Parties

interests of third parties

1.   The interests of the parties to a dispute and those of other Members under a covered agreement at issue in the dispute shall be fully taken into account during the panel process.

rights of third parties

2.   Any Member having a substantial interest in a matter before a panel and having notified its interest to the DSB (referred to in this Understanding as a "third party") shall have an opportunity to be heard by the panel and to make written submissions to the panel. These submissions shall also be given to the parties to the dispute and shall be reflected in the panel report.

3.   Third parties shall receive the submissions of the parties to the dispute to the first meeting of the panel.

separate dispute

4.   If a third party considers that a measure already the subject of a panel proceeding nullifies or impairs benefits accruing to it under any covered agreement, that Member may have recourse to normal dispute settlement procedures under this Understanding. Such a dispute shall be referred to the original panel wherever possible.

See also DSU 17.4 at p. 18 and Appdx 3:6 at p. 33.

Article 11
Function of Panels

findings to be made by panels

The function of panels is to assist the DSB in discharging its responsibilities under this Understanding and the covered agreements. Accordingly, a panel should make an objective assessment of the matter before it, including an objective assessment of the facts of the case and the applicability of and conformity with the relevant covered agreements, and make such other findings as will assist the DSB in making the recommendations or in giving the rulings provided for in the covered agreements. Panels should consult regularly with the parties to the dispute and give them adequate opportunity to develop a mutually satisfactory solution.

opportunity to develop a mutually satisfactory solution

Article 12

Panel Procedures

1.   Panels shall follow the Working Procedures in Appendix 3 unless the panel decides otherwise after consulting the parties to the dispute.

working procedures

2.   Panel procedures should provide sufficient flexibility so as to ensure high-quality panel reports, while not unduly delaying the panel process.

flexibility

3.   After consulting the parties to the dispute, the panelists shall, as soon as practicable and whenever possible within one week after the composition and terms of reference of the panel have been agreed upon, fix the timetable for the panel process, taking into account the provisions of paragraph 9 of Article 4, if relevant.

timetable

4.   In determining the timetable for the panel process, the panel shall provide sufficient time for the parties to the dispute to prepare their submissions.

time to prepare submissions

5.   Panels should set precise deadlines for written submissions by the parties and the parties should respect those deadlines.

deadlines

6.   Each party to the dispute shall deposit its written submissions with the Secretariat for immediate transmission to the panel and to the other party or parties to the dispute. The complaining party shall submit its first submission in advance of the responding party's first submission unless the panel decides, in fixing the timetable referred to in paragraph 3 and after consultations with the parties to the dispute, that the parties should submit their first submissions simultaneously. When there are sequential arrangements for the deposit of first submissions, the panel shall establish a firm time-period for receipt of the responding party's submission. Any subsequent written submissions shall be submitted simultaneously.

deposit of submissions

sequential submissions

7.   Where the parties to the dispute have failed to develop a mutually satisfactory solution, the panel shall submit its findings

content of panel report

in the form of a written report to the DSB. In such cases, the report of a panel shall set out the findings of fact, the applicability of relevant provisions and the basic rationale behind any findings and recommendations that it makes. Where a settlement of the matter among the parties to the dispute has been found, the report of the panel shall be confined to a brief description of the case and to reporting that a solution has been reached.

time period for examination

8. In order to make the procedures more efficient, the period in which the panel shall conduct its examination, from the date that the composition and terms of reference of the panel have been agreed upon until the date the final report is issued to the parties to the dispute, shall, as a general rule, not exceed six months. In cases of urgency, including those relating to perishable goods, the panel shall aim to issue its report to the parties to the dispute within three months.

See also DSU 20 at p. 20; SCM 4.12 at p. 60; GPA XXII:6 at p. 92.

extension of time period

9. When the panel considers that it cannot issue its report within six months, or within three months in cases of urgency, it shall inform the DSB in writing of the reasons for the delay together with an estimate of the period within which it will issue its report. In no case should the period from the establishment of the panel to the circulation of the report to the Members exceed nine months.

See also DSU 20 at p. 20; GPA XXII:6 at p. 92.

time period when developing countries are involved

10. In the context of consultations involving a measure taken by a developing country Member, the parties may agree to extend the periods established in paragraphs 7 and 8 of Article 4. If, after the relevant period has elapsed, the consulting parties cannot agree that the consultations have concluded, the Chairman of the DSB shall decide, after consultation with the parties, whether to extend the relevant period and, if so, for how long. In addition, in examining a complaint against a developing country Member, the panel shall accord sufficient time for the developing country Member to prepare and present its argumentation. The provisions of paragraph 1 of Article 20 and paragraph 4 of Article 21 are not affected by any action pursuant to this paragraph.

differential and more-favourable treatment

11. Where one or more of the parties is a developing country Member, the panel's report shall explicitly indicate the form in which account has been taken of relevant provisions on differential and more-favourable treatment for developing country Members that form part of the covered agreements which have been

raised by the developing country Member in the course of the dispute settlement procedures.

12.   The panel may suspend its work at any time at the request of the complaining party for a period not to exceed 12 months. In the event of such a suspension, the time-frames set out in paragraphs 8 and 9 of this Article, paragraph 1 of Article 20, and paragraph 4 of Article 21 shall be extended by the amount of time that the work was suspended. If the work of the panel has been suspended for more than 12 months, the authority for establishment of the panel shall lapse.

suspension of proceedings

Article 13

Right to Seek Information

1.   Each panel shall have the right to seek information and technical advice from any individual or body which it deems appropriate. However, before a panel seeks such information or advice from any individual or body within the jurisdiction of a Member it shall inform the authorities of that Member. A Member should respond promptly and fully to any request by a panel for such information as the panel considers necessary and appropriate. Confidential information which is provided shall not be revealed without formal authorization from the individual, body, or authorities of the Member providing the information.

conditions

2.   Panels may seek information from any relevant source and may consult experts to obtain their opinion on certain aspects of the matter. With respect to a factual issue concerning a scientific or other technical matter raised by a party to a dispute, a panel may request an advisory report in writing from an expert review group. Rules for the establishment of such a group and its procedures are set forth in Appendix 4.

experts

expert review group

See SPS 11 at p. 45; SCM 4.5 at p. 59; Customs Valuation 19 and Annex II at p. 57; TBT 14.2 and Annex 2 at p. 52.

Article 14

Confidentiality

1.   Panel deliberations shall be confidential.

panel deliberations

2.   The reports of panels shall be drafted without the presence of the parties to the dispute in the light of the information provided and the statements made.

drafting of panel report

anonymity
of opinions

3.   Opinions expressed in the panel report by individual panelists shall be anonymous.

See DSU 18 at p. 19 and CONFIDENTIALITY in the
Index.

Article 15

Interim Review Stage

submission of
descriptive
sections of report

1.   Following the consideration of rebuttal submissions and
oral arguments, the panel shall issue the descriptive (factual and
argument) sections of its draft report to the parties to the dispute.
Within a period of time set by the panel, the parties shall submit
their comments in writing.

submission of
interim report

2.   Following the expiration of the set period of time for receipt
of comments from the parties to the dispute, the panel shall issue
an interim report to the parties, including both the descriptive
sections and the panel's findings and conclusions. Within a period
of time set by the panel, a party may submit a written request for

request for review

the panel to review precise aspects of the interim report prior to
circulation of the final report to the Members. At the request of a
party, the panel shall hold a further meeting with the parties on the
issues identified in the written comments. If no comments are
received from any party within the comment period, the interim
report shall be considered the final panel report and circulated
promptly to the Members.

report on review

3.   The findings of the final panel report shall include a discus-
sion of the arguments made at the interim review stage. The

time period
for review

interim review stage shall be conducted within the time-period set
out in paragraph 8 of Article 12.

Article 16

Adoption of Panel Reports

minimum
time-period for
consideration
of reports

1.   In order to provide sufficient time for the Members to
consider panel reports, the reports shall not be considered for
adoption by the DSB until 20 days after the date they have been
circulated to the Members.

See also SCM 7.6 at p. 62.

objections

2.   Members having objections to a panel report shall give written
reasons to explain their objections for circulation at least 10 days prior
to the DSB meeting at which the panel report will be considered.

3.   The parties to a dispute shall have the right to participate fully in the consideration of the panel report by the DSB, and their views shall be fully recorded.

parties' participation

4.   Within 60 days after the date of circulation of a panel report to the Members, the report shall be adopted at a DSB meeting[7] unless a party to the dispute formally notifies the DSB of its decision to appeal or the DSB decides by consensus not to adopt the report. If a party has notified its decision to appeal, the report by the panel shall not be considered for adoption by the DSB until after completion of the appeal. This adoption procedure is without prejudice to the right of Members to express their views on a panel report.

adoption of report

Article 17

Appellate Review

Standing Appellate Body

1.   A standing Appellate Body shall be established by the DSB. The Appellate Body shall hear appeals from panel cases. It shall be composed of seven persons, three of whom shall serve on any one case. Persons serving on the Appellate Body shall serve in rotation. Such rotation shall be determined in the working procedures of the Appellate Body.

establishment

composition

rotation

2.   The DSB shall appoint persons to serve on the Appellate Body for a four-year term, and each person may be reappointed once. However, the terms of three of the seven persons appointed immediately after the entry into force of the WTO Agreement shall expire at the end of two years, to be determined by lot. Vacancies shall be filled as they arise. A person appointed to replace a person whose term of office has not expired shall hold office for the remainder of the predecessor's term.

appointment of members

3.   The Appellate Body shall comprise persons of recognized authority, with demonstrated expertise in law, international trade and the subject matter of the covered agreements generally. They shall be unaffiliated with any government. The Appellate Body membership shall be broadly representative of membership in the WTO. All persons serving on the Appellate Body shall be available at all times and on short notice, and shall stay abreast of

qualification of members

---

[7]   If a meeting of the DSB is not scheduled within this period at a time that enables the requirements of paragraphs 1 and 4 of Article 16 to be met, a meeting of the DSB shall be held for this purpose.

dispute settlement activities and other relevant activities of the WTO. They shall not participate in the consideration of any disputes that would create a direct or indirect conflict of interest.

right of appeal

4.　Only parties to the dispute, not third parties, may appeal a panel report. Third parties which have notified the DSB of a substantial interest in the matter pursuant to paragraph 2 of Article 10 may make written submissions to, and be given an opportunity to be heard by, the Appellate Body.

duration of proceedings

5.　As a general rule, the proceedings shall not exceed 60 days from the date a party to the dispute formally notifies its decision to appeal to the date the Appellate Body circulates its report. In fixing its timetable the Appellate Body shall take into account the provisions of paragraph 9 of Article 4, if relevant. When the Appellate Body considers that it cannot provide its report within 60 days, it shall inform the DSB in writing of the reasons for the delay together with an estimate of the period within which it will submit its report. In no case shall the proceedings exceed 90 days.

See also DSU 20 at p. 20 and SCM 4.9 at p. 60.

scope of appeal

6.　An appeal shall be limited to issues of law covered in the panel report and legal interpretations developed by the panel.

administrative and legal support

7.　The Appellate Body shall be provided with appropriate administrative and legal support as it requires.

expenses

8.　The expenses of persons serving on the Appellate Body, including travel and subsistence allowance, shall be met from the WTO budget in accordance with criteria to be adopted by the General Council, based on recommendations of the Committee on Budget, Finance and Administration.

Procedures for Appellate Review

working procedures

9.　Working procedures shall be drawn up by the Appellate Body in consultation with the Chairman of the DSB and the Director-General, and communicated to the Members for their information.

confidentiality

10.　The proceedings of the Appellate Body shall be confidential. The reports of the Appellate Body shall be drafted without the presence of the parties to the dispute and in the light of the information provided and the statements made.

anonymity of opinions

11.　Opinions expressed in the Appellate Body report by individuals serving on the Appellate Body shall be anonymous.

12.   The Appellate Body shall address each of the issues raised in accordance with paragraph 6 during the appellate proceeding.

scope of examination

13.   The Appellate Body may uphold, modify or reverse the legal findings and conclusions of the panel.

competence of Appellate Body

Adoption of Appellate Body Reports

14.   An Appellate Body report shall be adopted by the DSB and unconditionally accepted by the parties to the dispute unless the DSB decides by consensus not to adopt the Appellate Body report within 30 days following its circulation to the Members.[8] This adoption procedure is without prejudice to the right of Members to express their views on an Appellate Body report.

adoption of Appellate Body reports

See also SCM 4.9 at p. 60.

Article 18

Communications with the Panel or Appellate Body

1.   There shall be no *ex parte* communications with the panel or Appellate Body concerning matters under consideration by the panel or Appellate Body.

no ex parte communications

2.   Written submissions to the panel or the Appellate Body shall be treated as confidential, but shall be made available to the parties to the dispute. Nothing in this Understanding shall preclude a party to a dispute from disclosing statements of its own positions to the public. Members shall treat as confidential information submitted by another Member to the panel or the Appellate Body which that Member has designated as confidential. A party to a dispute shall also, upon request of a Member, provide a non-confidential summary of the information contained in its written submissions that could be disclosed to the public.

confidentiality

public disclosure of submissions

See CONFIDENTIALITY in the Index.

Article 19

Panel and Appellate Body Recommendations

1.   Where a panel or the Appellate Body concludes that a measure is inconsistent with a covered agreement, it shall recommend that the Member concerned[9] bring the measure into con-

recommendations

---

[8]   If a meeting of the DSB is not scheduled during this period, such a meeting of the DSB shall be held for this purpose.

[9]   The "Member concerned" is the party to the dispute to which the panel or Appellate Body recommendations are directed.

*suggestions on
implementation*

formity with that agreement.[10] In addition to its recommenda-tions, the panel or Appellate Body may suggest ways in which the Member concerned could implement the recommendations.

*rights and
obligations under
covered
agreements*

2.   In accordance with paragraph 2 of Article 3, in their findings and recommendations, the panel and Appellate Body cannot add to or diminish the rights and obligations provided in the covered agreements.

Article 20
Time-frame for DSB Decisions

time period

Unless otherwise agreed to by the parties to the dispute, the period from the date of establishment of the panel by the DSB until the date the DSB considers the panel or appellate report for adoption shall as a general rule not exceed nine months where the panel report is not appealed or 12 months where the report is appealed. Where either the panel or the Appellate Body has acted, pursuant to paragraph 9 of Article 12 or paragraph 5 of Article 17, to extend the time for providing its report, the additional time taken shall be added to the above periods.

See DSU 12.9, 12.10 at p. 14 ; SCM 4.12 and 8.5 at pp. 60, 63; GPA XXII:6 at p. 92.

Article 21
Surveillance of Implementation of Recommendations and Rulings

prompt compliance

1.   Prompt compliance with recommendations or rulings of the DSB is essential in order to ensure effective resolution of disputes to the benefit of all Members.

*developing
countries*

2.   Particular attention should be paid to matters affecting the interests of developing country Members with respect to measures which have been subject to dispute settlement.

*notification of
intentions in
respect of
implementation*

3.   At a DSB meeting held within 30 days[11] after the date of adoption of the panel or Appellate Body report, the Member concerned shall inform the DSB of its intentions in respect of implementation of the recommendations and rulings of the DSB.

[10]   With respect to recommendations in cases not involving a violation of GATT 1994 or any other covered agreement, see Article 26.

[11]   If a meeting of the DSB is not scheduled during this period, such a meeting of the DSB shall be held for this purpose.

If it is impracticable to comply immediately with the recommendations and rulings, the Member concerned shall have a reasonable period of time in which to do so. The reasonable period of time shall be: *reasonable period*

(a)   the period of time proposed by the Member concerned, provided that such period is approved by the DSB; or, in the absence of such approval, *approved by DSB*

(b)   a period of time mutually agreed by the parties to the dispute within 45 days after the date of adoption of the recommendations and rulings; or, in the absence of such agreement, *agreed by parties*

(c)   a period of time determined through binding arbitration within 90 days after the date of adoption of the recommendations and rulings.[12] In such arbitration, a guideline for the arbitrator[13] should be that the reasonable period of time to implement panel or Appellate Body recommendations should not exceed 15 months from the date of adoption of a panel or Appellate Body report. However, that time may be shorter or longer, depending upon the particular circumstances. *determined through binding arbitration*

4.   Except where the panel or the Appellate Body has extended, pursuant to paragraph 9 of Article 12 or paragraph 5 of Article 17, the time of providing its report, the period from the date of establishment of the panel by the DSB until the date of determination of the reasonable period of time shall not exceed 15 months unless the parties to the dispute agree otherwise. Where either the panel or the Appellate Body has acted to extend the time of providing its report, the additional time taken shall be added to the 15-month period; provided that unless the parties to the dispute agree that there are exceptional circumstances, the total time shall not exceed 18 months. *maximum duration until date of determination of reasonable period*

See also DSU 12.10 at p. 14; SCM 4.12 at p. 60; GPA XXII:6 at p. 92.

5.   Where there is disagreement as to the existence or consistency with a covered agreement of measures taken to comply with the recommendations and rulings such dispute shall be decided through recourse to these dispute settlement procedures, includ- *dispute on implementation*

[12]   If the parties cannot agree on an arbitrator within ten days after referring the matter to arbitration, the arbitrator shall be appointed by the Director-General within ten days, after consulting the parties.

[13]   The expression "arbitrator" shall be interpreted as referring either to an individual or a group.

referral to
original panel

ing wherever possible resort to the original panel. The panel shall circulate its report within 90 days after the date of referral of the matter to it. When the panel considers that it cannot provide its report within this time frame, it shall inform the DSB in writing of the reasons for the delay together with an estimate of the period within which it will submit its report.

See however GPA XXII:6 at p. 92.

surveillance by
DSB

6.   The DSB shall keep under surveillance the implementation of adopted recommendations or rulings. The issue of implementation of the recommendations or rulings may be raised at the DSB by any Member at any time following their adoption. Unless the DSB decides otherwise, the issue of implementation of the recommendations or rulings shall be placed on the agenda of the DSB meeting after six months following the date of establishment of the reasonable period of time pursuant to paragraph 3 and shall remain on the DSB's agenda until the issue is resolved. At least 10 days prior to each such DSB meeting, the Member concerned shall provide the DSB with a status report in writing of its progress in the implementation of the recommendations or rulings.

developing country

7.   If the matter is one which has been raised by a developing country Member, the DSB shall consider what further action it might take which would be appropriate to the circumstances.

8.   If the case is one brought by a developing country Member, in considering what appropriate action might be taken, the DSB shall take into account not only the trade coverage of measures complained of, but also their impact on the economy of developing country Members concerned.

Article 22

Compensation and the Suspension of Concessions

temporary
measures

1.   Compensation and the suspension of concessions or other obligations are temporary measures available in the event that the recommendations and rulings are not implemented within a reasonable period of time. However, neither compensation nor the suspension of concessions or other obligations is preferred to full implementation of a recommendation to bring a measure into conformity with the covered agreements. Compensation is voluntary and, if granted, shall be consistent with the covered agreements.

consistency of
compensation with
covered
agreements

See also DSU 26.1(b),(c),(d) at p. 29 and SCM. 4.10 at p. 60; GPA XXII:7 at p. 92.

2. If the Member concerned fails to bring the measure found to be inconsistent with a covered agreement into compliance therewith or otherwise comply with the recommendations and rulings within the reasonable period of time determined pursuant to paragraph 3 of Article 21, such Member shall, if so requested, and no later than the expiry of the reasonable period of time, enter into negotiations with any party having invoked the dispute settlement procedures, with a view to developing mutually acceptable compensation. If no satisfactory compensation has been agreed within 20 days after the date of expiry of the reasonable period of time, any party having invoked the dispute settlement procedures may request authorization from the DSB to suspend the application to the Member concerned of concessions or other obligations under the covered agreements.

negotiations on compensation

request for authorization to suspend obligations

3. In considering what concessions or other obligations to suspend, the complaining party shall apply the following principles and procedures:

principles for suspension of obligations

(a) the general principle is that the complaining party should first seek to suspend concessions or other obligations with respect to the same sector(s) as that in which the panel or Appellate Body has found a violation or other nullification or impairment;

same sector

(b) if that party considers that it is not practicable or effective to suspend concessions or other obligations with respect to the same sector(s), it may seek to suspend concessions or other obligations in other sectors under the same agreement;

other sectors under same agreement

(c) if that party considers that it is not practicable or effective to suspend concessions or other obligations with respect to other sectors under the same agreement, and that the circumstances are serious enough, it may seek to suspend concessions or other obligations under another covered agreement;

another covered agreement

See however GPA XXII:6 at p. 92.

(d) in applying the above principles, that party shall take into account:

(i) the trade in the sector or under the agreement under which the panel or Appellate Body has found a violation or other nullification or impairment, and the importance of such trade to that party;

affected trade in sector or agreement

broader economic elements and consequences	(ii)	the broader economic elements related to the nullification or impairment and the broader economic consequences of the suspension of concessions or other obligations;
request for suspension	(e)	if that party decides to request authorization to suspend concessions or other obligations pursuant to subparagraphs (b) or (c), it shall state the reasons therefore in its request. At the same time as the request is forwarded to the DSB, it also shall be forwarded to the relevant Councils and also, in the case of a request pursuant to subparagraph (b), the relevant sectoral bodies;
sector	(f)	for purposes of this paragraph, "sector" means:

sector (f) for purposes of this paragraph, "sector" means:

    (i) with respect to goods, all goods;

    (ii) with respect to services, a principal sector as identified in the current "Services Sectoral Classification List" which identifies such sectors;[14]

    (iii) with respect to trade-related intellectual property rights, each of the categories of intellectual property rights covered in Section 1, or Section 2, or Section 3, or Section 4, or Section 5, or Section 6, or Section 7 of Part II, or the obligations under Part III, or Part IV of the Agreement on TRIPS;

    (g) for purposes of this paragraph, "agreement" means:

agreement

    (i) with respect to goods, the agreements listed in Annex 1A of the WTO Agreement, taken as a whole as well as the Plurilateral Trade Agreements in so far as the relevant parties to the dispute are parties to these agreements;

    (ii) with respect to services, the GATS;

    (iii) with respect to intellectual property rights, the Agreement on TRIPS.

level of suspension   4.   The level of the suspension of concessions or other obligations authorized by the DSB shall be equivalent to the level of the nullification or impairment.

---

[14]   The list in document MTN.GNS/W/120 identifies eleven sectors: Business services; communication services; construction and related engineering services; distribution services; educational services; environmental services; financial services; health related and social services; tourism and travel related services; recreational, cultural and sporting services; and transport services.

5.   The DSB shall not authorize suspension of concessions or other obligations if a covered agreement prohibits such suspension.

prohibited suspensions

6.   When the situation described in paragraph 2 occurs, the DSB, upon request, shall grant authorization to suspend concessions or other obligations within 30 days of the expiry of the reasonable period of time unless the DSB decides by consensus to reject the request. However, if the Member concerned objects to the level of suspension proposed, or claims that the principles and procedures set forth in paragraph 3 have not been followed where a complaining party has requested authorization to suspend concessions or other obligations pursuant to paragraph 3(b) or (c), the matter shall be referred to arbitration. Such arbitration shall be carried out by the original panel, if members are available, or by an arbitrator[15] appointed by the Director-General and shall be completed within 60 days after the date of expiry of the reasonable period of time. Concessions or other obligations shall not be suspended during the course of the arbitration.

objections to level of suspension

referral to arbitration

See SCM 4.11 and 7.10 at pp. 60, 62.

7.   The arbitrator[16] acting pursuant to paragraph 6 shall not examine the nature of the concessions or other obligations to be suspended but shall determine whether the level of such suspension is equivalent to the level of nullification or impairment. The arbitrator may also determine if the proposed suspension of concessions or other obligations is allowed under the covered agreement. However, if the matter referred to arbitration includes a claim that the principles and procedures set forth in paragraph 3 have not been followed, the arbitrator shall examine that claim. In the event the arbitrator determines that those principles and procedures have not been followed, the complaining party shall apply them consistent with paragraph 3. The parties shall accept the arbitrator's decision as final and the parties concerned shall not seek a second arbitration. The DSB shall be informed promptly of the decision of the arbitrator and shall upon request, grant authorization to suspend concessions or other obligations where the request is consistent with the decision of the arbitrator, unless the DSB decides by consensus to reject the request.

object of arbitration

decision of arbitration final

DSB authorization to suspend

[15]   The expression "arbitrator" shall be interpreted as referring either to an individual or a group.

[16]   The expression "arbitrator" shall be interpreted as referring either to an individual or a group or to the members of the original panel when serving in the capacity of arbitrator.

temporary nature ***of suspension***	8. The suspension of concessions or other obligations shall be temporary and shall only be applied until such time as the measure found to be inconsistent with a covered agreement has been removed, or the Member that must implement recommendations or rulings provides a solution to the nullification or impairment of benefits, or a mutually satisfactory solution is reached. In accordance with para-
continued ***surveillance***	graph 6 of Article 21, the DSB shall continue to keep under surveil- lance the implementation of adopted recommendations or rulings, including those cases where compensation has been provided or concessions or other obligations have been suspended but the recom- mendations to bring a measure into conformity with the covered agreements have not been implemented.
measures by ***regional or local*** ***governments***	9. The dispute settlement provisions of the covered agree- ments may be invoked in respect of measures affecting their observance taken by regional or local governments or authorities within the territory of a Member. When the DSB has ruled that a provision of a covered agreement has not been observed, the responsible Member shall take such reasonable measures as may be available to it to ensure its observance. The provisions of the covered agreements and this Understanding relating to compen- sation and suspension of concessions or other obligations apply in cases where it has not been possible to secure such observance.[17]

See DSU 26 for enforcement of situation complaints at p. 28; GATS XXIII at p. 69.

Article 23

Strengthening of the Multilateral System

obligation to have ***recourse to DSU***	1. When Members seek the redress of a violation of obligations or other nullification or impairment of benefits under the covered agreements or an impediment to the attainment of any objective of the covered agreements, they shall have recourse to, and abide by, the rules and procedures of this Understanding.

2.   In such cases, Members shall:

    (a)   not make a determination to the effect that a violation has occurred, that benefits have been nullified or im- paired or that the attainment of any objective of the

---

[17]   Where the provisions of any covered agreement concerning measures taken by regional or local governments or authorities within the territory of a Member contain provisions different from the provisions of this paragraph, the provisions of such covered agreement shall prevail.

covered agreements has been impeded, except through recourse to dispute settlement in accordance with the rules and procedures of this Understanding, and shall make any such determination consistent with the findings contained in the panel or Appellate Body report adopted by the DSB or an arbitration award rendered under this Understanding;

determination that violation occurred, benefits have been impaired or attainment of objective impaired

(b)   follow the procedures set forth in Article 21 to determine the reasonable period of time for the Member concerned to implement the recommendations and rulings; and

determination of reasonable period of time for implementation

(c)   follow the procedures set forth in Article 22 to determine the level of suspension of concessions or other obligations and obtain DSB authorization in accordance with those procedures before suspending concessions or other obligations under the covered agreements in response to the failure of the Member concerned to implement the recommendations and rulings within that reasonable period of time.

determination of level of suspension

Article 24

Special Procedures Involving Least-Developed Country Members

1.   At all stages of the determination of the causes of a dispute and of dispute settlement procedures involving a least-developed country Member, particular consideration shall be given to the special situation of least-developed country Members. In this regard, Members shall exercise due restraint in raising matters under these procedures involving a least-developed country Member. If nullification or impairment is found to result from a measure taken by a least-developed country Member, complaining parties shall exercise due restraint in asking for compensation or seeking authorization to suspend the application of concessions or other obligations pursuant to these procedures.

consideration and due restraint

2.   In dispute settlement cases involving a least-developed country Member, where a satisfactory solution has not been found in the course of consultations the Director-General or the Chairman of the DSB shall, upon request by a least-developed country Member offer their good offices, conciliation and mediation with a view to assisting the parties to settle the dispute, before a request

good offices

for a panel is made. The Director-General or the Chairman of the DSB, in providing the above assistance, may consult any source which either deems appropriate.

Article 25

Arbitration

alternative means of dispute settlement

1.　Expeditious arbitration within the WTO as an alternative means of dispute settlement can facilitate the solution of certain disputes that concern issues that are clearly defined by both parties.

by mutual agreement notified to other Members

2.　Except as otherwise provided in this Understanding, resort to arbitration shall be subject to mutual agreement of the parties which shall agree on the procedures to be followed. Agreements to resort to arbitration shall be notified to all Members sufficiently in advance of the actual commencement of the arbitration process.

third parties

3.　Other Members may become party to an arbitration proceeding only upon the agreement of the parties which have agreed to have recourse to arbitration. The parties to the proceeding shall agree to abide by the arbitration award. Arbitration awards shall be notified to the DSB and the Council or Committee of any relevant agreement where any Member may raise any point relating thereto.

implementation, compensation and suspension

4.　Articles 21 and 22 of this Understanding shall apply *mutatis mutandis* to arbitration awards.

See references under ARBITRATION in the Index.

Article 26

1.　*Non-Violation Complaints of the Type Described in Paragraph 1(b) of Article XXIII of GATT 1994*

complaints on measures not inconsistent with the GATT 1994

Where the provisions of paragraph 1(b) of Article XXIII of GATT 1994 are applicable to a covered agreement, a panel or the Appellate Body may only make rulings and recommendations where a party to the dispute considers that any benefit accruing to it directly or indirectly under the relevant covered agreement is being nullified or impaired or the attainment of any objective of that Agreement is being impeded as a result of the application by a Member of any measure, whether or not it conflicts with the provisions of that Agreement. Where and to the extent that such party considers and a panel or the Appellate Body determines that a case concerns a measure that does not conflict with the provisions of a covered agreement to which the provisions of paragraph 1(b) of Article XXIII of GATT 1994 are applicable, the procedures in this Understanding shall apply, subject to the following:

(a) the complaining party shall present a detailed justification in support of any complaint relating to a measure which does not conflict with the relevant covered agreement;

detailed justification

(b) where a measure has been found to nullify or impair benefits under, or impede the attainment of objectives, of the relevant covered agreement without violation thereof, there is no obligation to withdraw the measure. However, in such cases, the panel or the Appellate Body shall recommend that the Member concerned make a mutually satisfactory adjustment;

no obligation to withdraw measure

(c) notwithstanding the provisions of Article 21, the arbitration provided for in paragraph 3 of Article 21, upon request of either party, may include a determination of the level of benefits which have been nullified or impaired, and may also suggest ways and means of reaching a mutually satisfactory adjustment; such suggestions shall not be binding upon the parties to the dispute;

determination of level of nullified or impaired benefits

(d) notwithstanding the provisions of paragraph 1 of Article 22, compensation may be part of a mutually satisfactory adjustment as final settlement of the dispute.

compensation as final settlement

2. *Complaints of the Type Described in Paragraph 1(c) of Article XXIII of GATT 1994*

Where the provisions of paragraph 1(c) of Article XXIII of GATT 1994 are applicable to a covered agreement, a panel may only make rulings and recommendations where a party considers that any benefit accruing to it directly or indirectly under the relevant covered agreement is being nullified or impaired or the attainment of any objective of that Agreement is being impeded as a result of the existence of any situation other than those to which the provisions of paragraphs 1(a) and 1(b) of Article XXIII of GATT 1994 are applicable. Where and to the extent that such party considers and a panel determines that the matter is covered by this paragraph, the procedures of this Understanding shall apply only up to and including the point in the proceedings where

complaints regarding other situations

applicable procedures

the panel report has been circulated to the Members. The dispute settlement rules and procedures contained in the Decision of 12 April 1989 (BISD 36S/61-67) shall apply to consideration for adoption, and surveillance and implementation of recommendations and rulings. The following shall also apply:

detailed
justification

(a)   the complaining party shall present a detailed justification in support of any argument made with respect to issues covered under this paragraph;

separate report

(b)   in cases involving matters covered by this paragraph, if a panel finds that cases also involve dispute settlement matters other than those covered by this paragraph, the panel shall circulate a report to the DSB addressing any such matters and a separate report on matters falling under this paragraph.

See the provisions of the Montreal Decision at p. 73.

Article 27

Responsibilities of the Secretariat

assistance and
support

1.   The Secretariat shall have the responsibility of assisting panels, especially on the legal, historical and procedural aspects of the matters dealt with, and of providing secretarial and technical support.

legal expert to
assist developing
countries

2.   While the Secretariat assists Members in respect of dispute settlement at their request, there may also be a need to provide additional legal advice and assistance in respect of dispute settlement to developing country Members. To this end, the Secretariat shall make available a qualified legal expert from the WTO technical cooperation services to any developing country Member which so requests. This expert shall assist the developing country Member in a manner ensuring the continued impartiality of the Secretariat.

training courses

3.   The Secretariat shall conduct special training courses for interested Members concerning these dispute settlement procedures and practices so as to enable Members' experts to be better informed in this regard.

See also DSU 8.4 at p. 10.

APPENDIX 1
AGREEMENTS COVERED BY THE UNDERSTANDING

(A)   Agreement Establishing the World Trade Organization

(B)   Multilateral Trade Agreements

Annex 1A: Multilateral Agreements on Trade in Goods

Annex 1B: General Agreement on Trade in Services

Annex 1C: Agreement on Trade-Related Aspects of Intellectual Property Rights

Annex 2:   Understanding on Rules and Procedures Governing the Settlement of Disputes

(C)   Plurilateral Trade Agreements

Annex 4:   Agreement on Trade in Civil Aircraft
Agreement on Government Procurement
International Dairy Agreement
International Bovine Meat Agreement

The applicability of this Understanding to the Plurilateral Trade Agreements shall be subject to the adoption of a decision by the parties to each agreement setting out the terms for the application of the Understanding to the individual agreement, including any special or additional rules or procedures for inclusion in Appendix 2, as notified to the DSB.

APPENDIX 2
SPECIAL OR ADDITIONAL RULES AND PROCEDURES CONTAINED IN THE COVERED AGREEMENTS

Agreement	Rules and Procedures
Agreement on the Application of Sanitary and Phytosanitary Measures	11.2
Agreement on Textiles and Clothing	2.14, 2.21, 4.4, 5.2, 5.4, 5.6, 6.9, 6.10, 6.11, 8.1 through 8.12
Agreement on Technical Barriers to Trade	14.2 through 14.4, Annex 2
Agreement on Implementation of Article VI of GATT 1994	17.4 through 17.7
Agreement on Implementation of Article VII of GATT 1994	19.3 through 19.5, Annex II.2(f), 3, 9, 21
Agreement on Subsidies and Countervailing Measures	4.2 through 4.12, 6.6, 7.2 through 7.10, 8.5, footnote 35, 24.4, 27.7, Annex V
General Agreement on Trade in Services	XXII:3, XXIII:3
Annex on Financial Services	4
Annex on Air Transport Services	4
Decision on Certain Dispute Settlement Procedures for the GATS	1 through 5

The list of rules and procedures in this Appendix includes provisions where only a part of the provision may be relevant in this context.

Any special or additional rules or procedures in the Plurilateral Trade Agreements as determined by the competent bodies of each agreement and as notified to the DSB.

APPENDIX 3
WORKING PROCEDURES

1.　In its proceedings the panel shall follow the relevant provisions of this Understanding. In addition, the following working procedures shall apply. *obligation to follow DSU*

2.　The panel shall meet in closed session. The parties to the dispute, and interested parties, shall be present at the meetings only when invited by the panel to appear before it. *closed session*

3.　The deliberations of the panel and the documents submitted to it shall be kept confidential. Nothing in this Understanding shall preclude a party to a dispute from disclosing statements of its own positions to the public. Members shall treat as confidential information submitted by another Member to the panel which that Member has designated as confidential. Where a party to a dispute submits a confidential version of its written submissions to the panel, it shall also, upon request of a Member, provide a non-confidential summary of the information contained in its submissions that could be disclosed to the public. *confidentiality*

4.　Before the first substantive meeting of the panel with the parties, the parties to the dispute shall transmit to the panel written submissions in which they present the facts of the case and their arguments. *written submissions*

5.　At its first substantive meeting with the parties, the panel shall ask the party which has brought the complaint to present its case. Subsequently, and still at the same meeting, the party against which the complaint has been brought shall be asked to present its point of view. *first meeting*

6.　All third parties which have notified their interest in the dispute to the DSB shall be invited in writing to present their views during a session of the first substantive meeting of the panel set aside for that purpose. All such third parties may be present during the entirety of this session. *third parties*

7.　Formal rebuttals shall be made at a second substantive meeting of the panel. The party complained against shall have the right to take the floor first to be followed by the complaining party. The parties shall submit, prior to that meeting, written rebuttals to the panel. *second meeting*

questions and
explanations

8.   The panel may at any time put questions to the parties and ask them for explanations either in the course of a meeting with the parties or in writing.

written version
of oral statements

9.   The parties to the dispute and any third party invited to present its views in accordance with Article 10 shall make available to the panel a written version of their oral statements.

transparency

10.   In the interest of full transparency, the presentations, rebuttals and statements referred to in paragraphs 5 to 9 shall be made in the presence of the parties. Moreover, each party's written submissions, including any comments on the descriptive part of the report and responses to questions put by the panel, shall be made available to the other party or parties.

additional
procedures

11.   Any additional procedures specific to the panel.

timetable

12.   Proposed timetable for panel work:

    (a)   Receipt of first written submissions of the parties:

        (1)   complaining Party: __   3-6 weeks

        (2)   Party complained against: __   2-3 weeks

    (b)   Date, time and place of first
        substantive meeting with the
        parties: third party session: __   1-2 weeks

    (c)   Receipt of written rebuttals
        of the parties: __   2-3 weeks

    (d)   Date, time and place of second
        substantive meeting with the
        parties: __   1-2 weeks

    (e)   Issuance of descriptive part of
        the report to the parties: __   2-4 weeks

    (f)   Receipt of comments by the
        parties on the descriptive
        part of the report: __   2 weeks

    (g)   Issuance of the interim report,
        including the findings and
        conclusions, to the parties: __   2-4 weeks

    (h)   Deadline for party to request
        review of part(s) of report: __   1 week

(i)	Period of review by panel, including possible additional meeting with parties:	—	2 weeks
(j)	Issuance of final report to parties to dispute:	—	2 weeks
(k)	Circulation of the final report to the Members:	—	3 weeks

The above calendar may be changed in the light of unforeseen developments. Additional meetings with the parties shall be scheduled if required.

modifications of timetable

APPENDIX 4
EXPERT REVIEW GROUPS

The following rules and procedures shall apply to expert review groups established in accordance with the provisions of paragraph 2 of Article 13.

under panel's authority

1. Expert review groups are under the panel's authority. Their terms of reference and detailed working procedures shall be decided by the panel, and they shall report to the panel.

qualifications of experts

2. Participation in expert review groups shall be restricted to persons of professional standing and experience in the field in question.

citizens of parties

3. Citizens of parties to the dispute shall not serve on an expert review group without the joint agreement of the parties to the dispute, except in exceptional circumstances when the panel considers that the need for specialized scientific expertise cannot be fulfilled otherwise. Government officials of parties to the dispute shall not serve on an expert review group. Members of expert review groups shall serve in their individual capacities and not as government representatives, nor as representatives of any organization. Governments or organizations shall therefore not give them instructions with regard to matters before an expert review group.

government officials of parties

independence

right to seek information and technical advice

4. Expert review groups may consult and seek information and technical advice from any source they deem appropriate. Before an expert review group seeks such information or advice from a source within the jurisdiction of a Member, it shall inform the government of that Member. Any Member shall respond promptly and fully to any request by an expert review group for such information as the expert review group considers necessary and appropriate.

access to information

5. The parties to a dispute shall have access to all relevant information provided to an expert review group, unless it is of a confidential nature. Confidential information provided to the expert review group shall not be released without formal authorization from the government, organization or person providing the information. Where such information is requested from the expert review group but release of such information by the expert review group is not authorized, a non-confidential summary of the information will be provided by the government, organization or person supplying the information.

6.   The expert review group shall submit a draft report to the parties to the dispute with a view to obtaining their comments, and taking them into account, as appropriate, in the final report, which shall also be issued to the parties to the dispute when it is submitted to the panel. The final report of the expert review group shall be advisory only.

report

See the various expert groups under specific agreements as indicated in the index under EXPERTS.

PROVISIONS ON CONSULTATIONS CONTAINED IN OTHER WTO AGREEMENTS AND REFERRED TO IN FOOTNOTE 4 OF ARTICLE 4.11 OF THE DSU

AGREEMENT ON AGRICULTURE

Article 19

Consultation and Dispute Settlement

The provisions of Articles XXII and XXIII of GATT 1994, as elaborated and applied by the Dispute Settlement Understanding, shall apply to consultations and the settlement of disputes under this Agreement.

AGREEMENT ON THE APPLICATION OF SANITARY AND PHYTOSANITARY MEASURES

Article 11

Consultations and Dispute Settlement

1.   The provisions of Articles XXII and XXIII of GATT 1994 as elaborated and applied by the Dispute Settlement Understanding shall apply to consultations and the settlement of disputes under this Agreement, except as otherwise specifically provided herein.

AGREEMENT ON TEXTILES AND CLOTHING

Article 8

...

4.   Members shall afford to each other adequate opportunity for consultations with respect to any matters affecting the operation of this Agreement.

AGREEMENT ON TECHNICAL BARRIERS TO TRADE

Article 14

Consultation and Dispute Settlement

14.1 Consultations and the settlement of disputes with respect to any matter affecting the operation of this Agreement shall take place under the auspices of the Dispute Settlement Body and shall follow, mutatis mutandis, the provisions of Articles XXII and XXIII of GATT 1994, as elaborated and applied by the Dispute Settlement Understanding.

AGREEMENT ON TRADE-RELATED INVESTMENT MEASURES

Article 8

Consultation and Dispute Settlement

The provisions of Article XXII and XXIII of GATT 1994, as elaborated and applied by the Dispute Settlement Understanding, shall apply to consultations and the settlement of disputes under this Agreement.

AGREEMENT ON IMPLEMENTATION OF ARTICLE VI OF THE GENERAL AGREEMENT ON TARIFFS AND TRADE 1994

Article 17

Consultation and Dispute Settlement

...

17.2 Each Member shall afford sympathetic consideration to, and shall afford adequate opportunity for consultation regarding, representations made by another Member with respect to any matter affecting the operation of this Agreement.

AGREEMENT ON IMPLEMENTATION OF ARTICLE VII OF THE GENERAL AGREEMENT ON TARIFFS AND TRADE 1994

Article 19

Consultations and Dispute Settlement

[1.   Except as otherwise provided herein, the Dispute Settlement Understanding is applicable to consultations and the settlement of disputes under this Agreement.]

Paragraph 1 of Art. 19 is not referred to in Appendix 2 of DSU.

2.   If any Member considers that any benefit accruing to it, directly or indirectly, under this Agreement is being nullified or impaired, or that the achievement of any objective of this Agreement is being impeded, as a result of the actions of another member or of other members, it may, with a view to reaching a mutually satisfactory solution of this matter, request consultations with the Member or members in question. Each Member shall afford sympathetic consideration to any request from another member for consultations.

AGREEMENT ON PRESHIPMENT INSPECTION

Article 7

Consultation

Members shall consult with other Members upon request with respect to any matter affecting the operation of this Agreement. In such cases, the provisions of Article XXII of GATT 1994, as elaborated and applied by the Dispute Settlement Understanding, are applicable to this Agreement.

AGREEMENT ON RULES OF ORIGIN

Article 7

Consultation

The provisions of Article XXII of GATT 1994, as elaborated and applied by the Dispute Settlement Understanding, are applicable to this Agreement.

AGREEMENT ON IMPORT LICENSING PROCEDURES

Article 6

Consultation and Dispute Settlement

Consultations and the settlement of disputes with respect to any matter affecting the operation of this Agreement shall be subject to the provisions of Articles XXII and XXIII of GATT 1994, as elaborated and applied by the Dispute Settlement Understanding.

AGREEMENT ON SUBSIDIES AND COUNTERVAILING MEASURES

PART X: DISPUTE SETTLEMENT

Article 30

The provisions of Articles XXII and XXIII of GATT 1994 as elaborated and applied by the Dispute Settlement Understanding shall apply to consultations and the settlement of disputes under this Agreement, except as otherwise specifically provided herein.

AGREEMENT ON SAFEGUARDS

Article 14

Dispute Settlement

The provisions of Articles XXII and XXIII of GATT 1994 as elaborated and applied by the Dispute Settlement Understanding shall apply to consultations and the settlement of disputes arising under this Agreement.

See also GATT 1994 XXII:1 and XXIII:1 at p. 43; SCM 4.3. 7.2 and 7.3 at pp. 59 and 61; GATS XXII at p. 68; TRIPS 64 at p. 72; GPA XXII at p. 91; Aircraft 8.5 at p. 93; Dairy IV:5 at p. 95.

DECISION ON THE APPLICATION AND REVIEW OF THE UNDERSTANDING ON RULES AND PROCEDURES GOVERNING THE SETTLEMENT OF DISPUTES

Ministers,

Recalling the Decision of 22 February 1994 that existing rules and procedures of GATT 1947 in the field of dispute settlement shall remain in effect until the date of entry into force of the Agreement Establishing the World Trade Organization,

Invite the relevant Councils and Committees to decide that they shall remain in operation for the purpose of dealing with any dispute for which the request for consultation was made before that date;

Invite the Ministerial Conference to complete a full review of dispute settlement rules and procedures under the World Trade Organization within four years after the entry into force of the Agreement Establishing the World Trade Organization, and to take a decision on the occasion of its first meeting after the completion of the review, whether to continue, modify or terminate such dispute settlement rules and procedures.

Article XXII of GATT 1994

Consultation

1.   Each contracting party shall accord sympathetic considera- *adequate*
tion to, and shall afford adequate opportunity for consultation *opportunity for*
regarding, such representations as may be made by another *consultations*
contracting party with respect to any matter affecting the operation
of this Agreement.

2.   The CONTRACTING PARTIES may, at the request of a *referral to*
contracting party, consult with any contracting party or parties in *CONTRACTING*
respect of any matter for which it has not been possible to find a *PARTIES*
satisfactory solution through consultation under paragraph 1.

Article XXIII of GATT 1994

Nullification or Impairment

1.   If any contracting party should consider that any benefit *nullification or*
accruing to it directly or indirectly under this Agreement is being *impairment*
nullified or impaired or that the attainment of any objective of the
Agreement is being impeded as the result of:

(a)   the failure of another contracting party to carry out its *violation*
obligations under this Agreement, or

(b)   the application by another contracting party of any
measure, whether or not it conflicts with the provisions
of this Agreement, or

(c)   the existence of any other situation, *other situation*

the contracting party may, with a view to the satisfactory adjust- *representation*
ment of the matter, make written representations or proposals to *or proposals*
the other contracting party or parties which it considers to be
concerned. Any contracting party thus approached shall give
sympathetic consideration to the representations or proposals
made to it.

2.   If no satisfactory adjustment is effected between the con- *referral to*
tracting parties concerned within a reasonable time, or if the *CONTRACTING*
difficulty is of the type described in paragraph 1(c) of this Article, *PARTIES*
the matter may be referred to the CONTRACTING PARTIES. The
CONTRACTING PARTIES shall promptly investigate any mat- *investigation*
ter so referred to them and shall make appropriate recommendations to the contracting parties which they consider to be con- *recommendations*
cerned, or give a ruling on the matter, as appropriate. The *or rulings*
CONTRACTING PARTIES may consult with contracting par-

authorization to suspend application of obligations

ties, with the Economic and Social Council of the United Nations and with any appropriate intergovernmental organization in cases where they consider such consultation necessary. If the CONTRACTING PARTIES consider that the circumstances are serious enough to justify such action, they may authorize a contracting party or parties to suspend the application to any other contracting party or parties of such concessions or other obligations under this Agreement as they determine to be appropriate in the circumstances. If the application to any contracting party of any concession or other obligation is in fact suspended, that contracting party shall then be free, not later than sixty days after such action is taken, to give written notice to the Executive Secretary[1] to the CONTRACTING PARTIES of its intention to

withdrawal

withdraw from this Agreement and such withdrawal shall take effect upon the sixtieth day following the day on which such notice is received by him.

---

[1]   By the Decision of 23 March 1965, the CONTRACTING PARTIES changed the title of the head of the GATT secretariat from "Executive Secretary" to "Director-General".

AGREEMENT ON THE APPLICATION OF SANITARY AND PHYTOSANITARY MEASURES

Article 11

Consultations and Dispute Settlement

...

2.   In a dispute under this Agreement involving scientific or technical issues, a panel should seek advice from experts chosen by the panel in consultation with the parties to the dispute. To this end, the panel may, when it deems it appropriate, establish an advisory technical experts group, or consult the relevant international organizations, at the request of either party to the dispute or on its own initiative.

advisory technical experts group

AGREEMENT ON TEXTILES AND CLOTHING

Article 2

...

14.   Except where the Council for Trade in Goods or the Dispute Settlement Body decides otherwise under paragraph 12 of Article 8, the level of each remaining restriction shall be increased annually during subsequent stages of this Agreement by not less than the following:

quota growth

    (a)   for Stage 2 (from the 37th to the 84th month that the WTO Agreement is in effect, inclusive), the growth rate for the respective restrictions during Stage 1, increased by 25 per cent;

    (b)   for Stage 3 (from the 85th to the 120th month that the WTO Agreement is in effect, inclusive), the growth rate for the respective restrictions during Stage 2, increased by 27 per cent.

...

TMB review of, and appropriate recommendations or findings on, the implementation of Article 2

21.   The TMB shall keep under review the implementation of this Article. It shall, at the request of any Member, review any particular matter with reference to the implementation of the provisions of this Article. It shall make appropriate recommendations or findings within 30 days to the Member or Members concerned, after inviting the participation of such Members.

Article 4

...

consultation on changes in the administration of restrictions

4.   When changes mentioned in paragraphs 2 and 3 are necessary, however, Members agree that the Member initiating such changes shall inform and, wherever possible, initiate consultations with the affected Member or Members prior to the implementation of such changes, with a view to reaching a mutually acceptable solution regarding appropriate and equitable adjustment. Members further agree that where consultation prior to implementation is not feasible, the Member initiating such changes will, at the request of the affected Member, consult, within 60 days if possible, with the Members concerned with a view to reaching a mutually satisfactory solution regarding appropriate and equitable adjustments. If a mutually

satisfactory solution is not reached, any Member involved may refer the matter to the TMB for recommendations as provided in Article 8. Should the TSB not have had the opportunity to review a dispute concerning such changes introduced prior to the entry into force of the WTO Agreement, it shall be reviewed by the TMB in accordance with the rules and procedures of the MFA applicable for such a review.

matter may be referred to TMB for recommendations

Article 5

...

2.   Should any Member believe that this Agreement is being circumvented by transshipment, re-routing, false declaration concerning country or place of origin, or falsification of official documents, and that no, or inadequate, measures are being applied to address and/or to take action against such circumvention, that Member should consult with the Member or Members concerned with a view to seeking a mutually satisfactory solution. Such consultations should be held promptly, and within 30 days when possible. If a mutually satisfactory solution is not reached, the matter may be referred by any Member involved to the TMB for recommendations.

consultation on circumvention of the Agreement

referral to TMB for recommendations

...

4.   Where, as a result of investigation, there is sufficient evidence that circumvention has occurred (e.g. where evidence is available concerning the country or place of true origin, and the circumstances of such circumvention), Members agree that appropriate action, to the extent necessary to address the problem, should be taken. Such action may include the denial of entry of goods or, where goods have entered, having due regard to the actual circumstances and the involvement of the country or place of true origin, the adjustment of charges to restraint levels to reflect the true country or place of origin. Also, where there is evidence of the involvement of the territories of the Members through which the goods have been transshipped, such action may include the introduction of restraints with respect to such Members. Any such actions, together with their timing and scope, may be taken after consultations held with a view to arriving at a mutually satisfactory solution between the concerned Members and shall be notified to the TMB with full justification. The Members concerned may agree on other remedies in

actions to address circumvention

denial of entry, adjustment of charges to restraint levels, restraints in case of transhipment

any actions to be notified to TMB

prompt review and recommendations by TMB

consultation. Any such agreement shall also be notified to the TMB, and the TMB may make such recommendations to the Members concerned as it deems appropriate. If a mutually satisfactory solution is not reached, any Member concerned may refer the matter to the TMB for prompt review and recommendations.

...

action to address false declarations made for the purposes of circumvention

6.   Members agree that false declaration concerning fibre content, quantities, description or classification of merchandise also frustrates the objective of this Agreement. Where there is evidence that any such false declaration has been made for purposes of circumvention, Members agree that appropriate measures, consistent with domestic laws and procedures, should be taken against the exporters or importers involved. Should any Member believe that this Agreement is being circumvented by such false declaration and that no, or inadequate, administrative measures are being applied to address and/or to take action against such circumvention, that Member should consult promptly with the Member involved with a view to seeking a mutually satisfactory solution. If such a solution is not reached, the matter may be referred by any Member involved to the TMB for recommendations. This provision is not intended to prevent Members from making technical adjustments when inadvertent errors in declarations have been made.

matter may be referred to TMB for recommendations

Article 6

...

agreed restraint measures under the transitional safeguard clause

9.   Details of the agreed restraint measure shall be communicated to the TMB within 60 days from the date of conclusion of the agreement. The TMB shall determine whether the agreement is justified in accordance with the provisions of this Article. In order to make its determination, the TMB shall have available to it the factual data provided to the Chairman of the TMB, referred to in paragraph 7, as well as any other relevant information provided by the Members concerned. The TMB may make such recommendations as it deems appropriate to the Members concerned.

review by TMB with recommendations if appropriate

introduction of restraint measures without agreement

10.   If, however, after the expiry of the period of 60 days from the date on which the request for consultations was received, there has been no agreement between the Members, the Member which proposed to take safeguard action may apply the restraint by date of import or date of export, in accordance with the provisions of

this Article, within 30 days following the 60-day period for consultations, and at the same time refer the matter to the TMB. It shall be open to either Member to refer the matter to the TMB before the expiry of the period of 60 days. In either case, the TMB shall promptly conduct an examination of the matter, including the determination of serious damage, or actual threat thereof, and its causes, and make appropriate recommendations to the Members concerned within 30 days. In order to conduct such examination, the TMB shall have available to it the factual data provided to the Chairman of the TMB, referred to in paragraph 7, as well as any other relevant information provided by the Members concerned.

referral to TMB

prompt examination and appropriate recommendations

11. In highly unusual and critical circumstances, where delay would cause damage which would be difficult to repair, action under paragraph 10 may be taken provisionally on the condition that the request for consultations and notification to the TMB shall be effected within no more than five working days after taking the action. In the case that consultations do not produce agreement, the TMB shall be notified at the conclusion of consultations, but in any case no later than 60 days from the date of the implementation of the action. The TMB shall promptly conduct an examination of the matter, and make appropriate recommendations to the Members concerned within 30 days. In the case that consultations do produce agreement, Members shall notify the TMB upon conclusion but, in any case, no later than 90 days from the date of the implementation of the action. The TMB may make such recommendations as it deems appropriate to the Members concerned.

provisional measure in highly unusual and critical circumstances

notification to TMB
prompt examination

appropriate recommendations

Article 8

1. In order to supervise the implementation of this Agreement, to examine all measures taken under this Agreement and their conformity therewith, and to take the actions specifically required of it by this Agreement, the Textiles Monitoring Body ("TMB") is hereby established. The TMB shall consist of a Chairman and 10 members. Its membership shall be balanced and broadly representative of the Members and shall provide for rotation of its members at appropriate intervals. The members shall be appointed by Members designated by the Council for Trade in Goods to serve on the TMB, discharging their function on an *ad personam* basis.

competence of the TMB

membership

2. The TMB shall develop its own working procedures. It is understood, however, that consensus within the TMB does not require

working procedures

the assent or concurrence of members appointed by Members involved in an unresolved issue under review by the TMB.

TMB as a
standing body

3.   The TMB shall be considered as a standing body and shall meet as necessary to carry out the functions required of it under this Agreement. It shall rely on notifications and information

TMB shall rely on
information,
notifications,
reports

supplied by the Members under the relevant Articles of this Agreement, supplemented by any additional information or necessary details they may submit or it may decide to seek from them. It may also rely on notifications to and reports from other WTO bodies and from such other sources as it may deem appropriate.

consultations

4.   Members shall afford to each other adequate opportunity for consultations with respect to any matters affecting the operation of this Agreement.

prompt
consideration

recommendations

5.   In the absence of any mutually agreed solution in the bilateral consultations provided for in this Agreement, the TMB shall, at the request of either Member, and following a thorough and prompt consideration of the matter, make recommendations to the Members concerned.

prompt review

obligation to enter
into consultations
before review

appropriate
observations

6.   At the request of any Member, the TMB shall review promptly any particular matter which that Member considers to be detrimental to its interests under this Agreement and where consultations between it and the Member or Members concerned have failed to produce a mutually satisfactory solution. On such matters, the TMB may make such observations as it deems appropriate to the Members concerned and for the purposes of the review provided for in paragraph 11.

participation of
directly affected
Members

7.   Before formulating its recommendations or observations, the TMB shall invite participation of such Members as may be directly affected by the matter in question.

recommendations
preferably within
30 days

8.   Whenever the TMB is called upon to make recommendations or findings, it shall do so, preferably within a period of 30 days, unless a different time period is specified in this Agreement. All such recommendations or findings shall be communicated to the Members directly concerned. All such recommendations or findings shall also be communicated to the Council for Trade in Goods for its information.

acceptance of
recommendation
and surveillance of
implementation

9.   The Members shall endeavour to accept in full the recommendations of the TMB, which shall exercise proper surveillance of the implementation of such recommendations.

10. If a Member considers itself unable to conform with the recommendations of the TMB, it shall provide the TMB with the reasons therefore not later than one month after receipt of such recommendations. Following thorough consideration of the reasons given, the TMB shall issue any further recommendations it considers appropriate forthwith. If, after such further recommendations, the matter remains unresolved, either Member may bring the matter before the Dispute Settlement Body and invoke paragraph 2 of Article XXIII of GATT 1994 and the relevant provisions of the Dispute Settlement Understanding.

non-conformance: reasons to be given

referral to DSB

11. In order to oversee the implementation of this Agreement, the Council for Trade in Goods shall conduct a major review before the end of each stage of the integration process. To assist in this review, the TMB shall, at least five months before the end of each stage, transmit to the Council for Trade in Goods a comprehensive report on the implementation of this Agreement during the stage under review, in particular in matters with regard to the integration process, the application of the transitional safeguard mechanism, and relating to the application of GATT 1994 rules and disciplines as defined in Articles 2, 3, 6 and 7 respectively. The TMB's comprehensive report may include any recommendation as deemed appropriate by the TMB to the Council for Trade in Goods.

major review by the Council for Trade in Goods before end of each stage

12. In the light of its review the Council for Trade in Goods shall by consensus take such decisions as it deems appropriate to ensure that the balance of rights and obligations embodied in this Agreement is not being impaired. For the resolution of any disputes that may arise with respect to matters referred to in Article 7, the Dispute Settlement Body may authorize, without prejudice to the final date set out under Article 9, an adjustment to paragraph 14 of Article 2, for the stage subsequent to the review, with respect to any Member found not to be complying with its obligations under this Agreement.

balance of rights and obligations: the CTG's role

The DSB's role if disputes arise on matters referred in Article 7

AGREEMENT ON TECHNICAL BARRIERS TO TRADE

Article 14
Consultation and Dispute Settlement

...

technical expert group

14.2 At the request of a party to a dispute, or at its own initiative, a panel may establish a technical expert group to assist in questions of a technical nature, requiring detailed consideration by experts.

procedures

14.3 Technical expert groups shall be governed by the procedures of Annex 2.

measures by local government, non-governmental and regional bodies

14.4 The dispute settlement provisions set out above can be invoked in cases where a Member considers that another Member has not achieved satisfactory results under Articles 3, 4, 7, 8 and 9 and its trade interests are significantly affected. In this respect, such results shall be equivalent to those as if the body in question were a Member.

ANNEX 2
TECHNICAL EXPERT GROUPS

The following procedures shall apply to technical expert groups established in accordance with the provisions of Article 14.

under panel's authority

1. Technical expert groups are under the panel's authority. Their terms of reference and detailed working procedures shall be decided by the panel, and they shall report to the panel.

qualification of experts

2. Participation in technical expert groups shall be restricted to persons of professional standing and experience in the field in question.

citizens of parties

3. Citizens of parties to the dispute shall not serve on a technical expert group without the joint agreement of the parties to the dispute, except in exceptional circumstances when the panel

government officials of parties

considers that the need for specialized scientific expertise cannot be fulfilled otherwise. Government officials of parties to the dispute shall not serve on a technical expert group. Members of technical

independence

expert groups shall serve in their individual capacities and not as government representatives, nor as representatives of any organization. Governments or organizations shall therefore not give them instructions with regard to matters before a technical expert group.

4.   Technical expert groups may consult and seek information and technical advice from any source they deem appropriate. Before a technical expert group seeks such information or advice from a source within the jurisdiction of a Member, it shall inform the government of that Member. Any Member shall respond promptly and fully to any request by a technical expert group for such information as the technical expert group considers necessary and appropriate.

right to seek information and technical advice

5.   The parties to a dispute shall have access to all relevant information provided to a technical expert group, unless it is of a confidential nature. Confidential information provided to the technical expert group shall not be released without formal authorization from the government, organization or person providing the information. Where such information is requested from the technical expert group but release of such information by the technical expert group is not authorized, a non-confidential summary of the information will be provided by the government, organization or person supplying the information.

access to information

6.   The technical expert group shall submit a draft report to the Members concerned with a view to obtaining their comments, and taking them into account, as appropriate, in the final report, which shall also be circulated to the Members concerned when it is submitted to the panel.

report

AGREEMENT ON IMPLEMENTATION OF
ARTICLE VI OF THE GENERAL AGREEMENT
ON TARIFFS AND TRADE 1994

Article 17
Consultation and Dispute Settlement

...

referral to DSB

17.4 If the Member that requested consultations considers that the consultations pursuant to paragraph 3 have failed to achieve a mutually agreed solution, and if final action has been taken by the administering authorities of the importing Member to levy definitive anti-dumping duties or to accept price undertakings, it may refer the matter to the Dispute Settlement Body ("DSB"). When a provisional measure has a significant impact and the Member that requested consultations considers that the measure was taken contrary to the provisions of paragraph 1 of Article 7, that Member may also refer such matter to the DSB.

establishment of panel

17.5 The DSB shall, at the request of the complaining party, establish a panel to examine the matter based upon:

basis for panel's examination of matter

(i) a written statement of the Member making the request indicating how a benefit accruing to it, directly or indirectly, under this Agreement has been nullified or impaired, or that the achieving of the objectives of the Agreement is being impeded, and

(ii) the facts made available in conformity with appropriate domestic procedures to the authorities of the importing Member.

17.6 In examining the matter referred to in paragraph 5:

standard for assessment of facts by panel

(i) in its assessment of the facts of the matter, the panel shall determine whether the authorities' establishment of the facts was proper and whether their evaluation of those facts was unbiased and objective. If the establishment of the facts was proper and the evaluation was unbiased and objective, even though the panel might have reached a different conclusion, the evaluation shall not be overturned;

(ii) the panel shall interpret the relevant provisions of the Agreement in accordance with customary rules of interpretation of public international law. Where the panel finds that a relevant provision of the Agreement admits of more than one permissible interpretation, the panel shall find the authorities' measure to be in conformity with the Agreement if it rests upon one of those permissible interpretations.

standard for interpretation of agreement by panel

See also the Decision on Review at p. 56.

17.7 Confidential information provided to the panel shall not be disclosed without formal authorization from the person, body or authority providing such information. Where such information is requested from the panel but release of such information by the panel is not authorized, a non-confidential summary of the information, authorized by the person, body or authority providing the information, shall be provided.

non-disclosure of confidential information

DECISION ON REVIEW OF ARTICLE 17.6 OF THE AGREEMENT ON IMPLEMENTATION OF ARTICLE VI OF THE GENERAL AGREEMENT ON TARIFFS AND TRADE 1994

Ministers decide as follows:

review after three years

The standard of review in paragraph 6 of Article 17 of the Agreement on Implementation of Article VI of GATT 1994 shall be reviewed after a period of three years with a view to considering the question of whether it is capable of general application.

AGREEMENT ON IMPLEMENTATION OF ARTICLE VII OF THE GENERAL AGREEMENT ON TARIFFS AND TRADE 1994

Article 19

Consultations and Dispute Settlement

...

3.　The Technical Committee shall provide, upon request, advice and assistance to Members engaged in consultations.

Technical Committee

4.　At the request of a party to the dispute, or on its own initiative, a panel established to examine a dispute relating to the provisions of this Agreement may request the Technical Committee to carry out an examination of any questions requiring technical consideration. The panel shall determine the terms of reference of the Technical Committee for the particular dispute and set a time period for receipt of the report of the Technical Committee. The panel shall take into consideration the report of the Technical Committee. In the event that the Technical Committee is unable to reach consensus on a matter referred to it pursuant to this paragraph, the panel should afford the parties to the dispute an opportunity to present their views on the matter to the panel.

request for examination

terms of reference and time period for receipt of report

5.　Confidential information provided to the panel shall not be disclosed without formal authorization from the person, body or authority providing such information. Where such information is requested from the panel but release of such information by the panel is not authorized, a non-confidential summary of this information, authorized by the person, body or authority providing the information, shall be provided.

confidential information

ANNEX II
TECHNICAL COMMITTEE ON CUSTOMS VALUATION

...

2.　The responsibilities of the Technical Committee shall include the following:

responsibilities

...

(f)　to carry out an examination of a matter referred to it by a panel under Article 19 of this Agreement; and

referral by panels

General

duration of work

3.   The Technical Committee shall attempt to conclude its work on specific matters, especially those referred to it by Members, the Committee or a panel, in a reasonably short period of time. As provided in paragraph 4 of Article 19, a panel shall set a specific time period for receipt of a report of the Technical Committee and the Technical Committee shall provide its report within that period.

...

Technical Committee Meetings

meetings

9.   The Technical Committee shall meet as necessary but at least two times a year. The date of each meeting shall be fixed by the Technical Committee at its preceding session. The date of the meeting may be varied either at the request of any member of the Technical Committee concurred in by a simple majority of the members of the Technical Committee or, in cases requiring urgent attention, at the request of the Chairman. Notwithstanding the provisions in sentence 1 of this paragraph, the Technical Commit-

referrals by panels

tee shall meet as necessary to consider matters referred to it by a panel under the provisions of Article 19 of this Agreement.

...

Quorum and Voting

decisions

21.   Each member of the Technical Committee shall have one vote. A decision of the Technical Committee shall be taken by a majority comprising at least two thirds of the members present. Regardless of the outcome of the vote on a particular matter, the Technical Committee shall be free to make a full report to the Committee and to the CCC on that matter indicating the different views expressed in the relevant discussions. Notwithstanding the

**matter referred
by panel**

above provisions of this paragraph, on matters referred to it by a panel, the Technical Committee shall take decisions by consensus. Where no agreement is reached in the Technical Committee on the question referred to it by a panel, the Technical Committee shall provide a report detailing the facts of the matter and indicating the views of the members.

AGREEMENT ON SUBSIDIES AND COUNTERVAILING MEASURES

PART II: PROHIBITED SUBSIDIES

Article 4
Remedies

...

4.2   A request for consultations under paragraph 1 shall include a statement of available evidence with regard to the existence and nature of the subsidy in question.

request for consultation

See however SCM 27.7 at p. 64

4.3   Upon request for consultations under paragraph 1, the Member believed to be granting or maintaining the subsidy in question shall enter into such consultations as quickly as possible. The purpose of the consultations shall be to clarify the facts of the situation and to arrive at a mutually agreed solution.

obligation to enter into consultation

4.4   If no mutually agreed solution has been reached within 30 days[1] of the request for consultations, any Member party to such consultations may refer the matter to the Dispute Settlement Body ("DSB") for the immediate establishment of a panel, unless the DSB decides by consensus not to establish a panel.

referral to DSB for establishment of panel

4.5   Upon its establishment, the panel may request the assistance of the Permanent Group of Experts[2] (referred to in this Agreement as the "PGE") with regard to whether the measure in question is a prohibited subsidy. If so requested, the PGE shall immediately review the evidence with regard to the existence and nature of the measure in question and shall provide an opportunity for the Member applying or maintaining the measure to demonstrate that the measure in question is not a prohibited subsidy. The PGE shall report its conclusions to the panel within a time-limit determined by the panel. The PGE's conclusions on the issue of whether or not the measure in question is a prohibited subsidy shall be accepted by the panel without modification.

Permanent Group of Experts

4.6   The panel shall submit its final report to the parties to the dispute. The report shall be circulated to all Members within

submission and circulation of panel report

---

[1]   Any time-periods mentioned in this Article may be extended by mutual agreement.

[2]   As established in Article 24.

90 days of the date of the composition and the establishment of the panel's terms of reference.

prohibited subsidies - panel recommendation

4.7   If the measure in question is found to be a prohibited subsidy, the panel shall recommend that the subsidizing Member withdraw the subsidy without delay. In this regard, the panel shall specify in its recommendation the time-period within which the measure must be withdrawn.

adoption of report

4.8   Within 30 days of the issuance of the panel's report to all Members, the report shall be adopted by the DSB unless one of the parties to the dispute formally notifies the DSB of its decision to appeal or the DSB decides by consensus not to adopt the report.

appeal

4.9   Where a panel report is appealed, the Appellate Body shall issue its decision within 30 days from the date when the party to the dispute formally notifies its intention to appeal. When the Appellate Body considers that it cannot provide its report within 30 days, it shall inform the DSB in writing of the reasons for the delay together with an estimate of the period within which it will submit its report. In no case shall the proceedings exceed 60 days. The appellate report shall be adopted by the DSB and unconditionally accepted by the parties to the dispute unless the DSB decides by consensus not to adopt the appellate report within 20 days following its issuance to the Members.[3]

See DSU 17.4, 17.5 at pp. 18, 19.

countermeasures

4.10   In the event the recommendation of the DSB is not followed within the time-period specified by the panel, which shall commence from the date of adoption of the panel's report or the Appellate Body's report, the DSB shall grant authorization to the complaining Member to take appropriate[4] countermeasures, unless the DSB decides by consensus to reject the request.

arbitration

4.11   In the event a party to the dispute requests arbitration under paragraph 6 of Article 22 of the Dispute Settlement Understanding ("DSU"), the arbitrator shall determine whether the countermeasures are appropriate.[5]

time periods

4.12   For purposes of disputes conducted pursuant to this Article, except for time periods specifically prescribed in this Article,

---

[3]   If a meeting of the DSB is not scheduled during this period, such a meeting shall be held for this purpose.

[4]   This expression is not meant to allow countermeasures that are disproportionate in light of the fact that the subsidies dealt with under these provisions are prohibited.

[5]   This expression is not meant to allow countermeasures that are disproportionate in light of the fact that the subsidies dealt with under these provisions are prohibited.

time-periods applicable under the DSU for the conduct of such disputes shall be half the time prescribed therein.

See SCM 27.7 for Developing Country at p. 64.

PART III: ACTIONABLE SUBSIDIES

Article 6
Serious Prejudice

...

6.6   Each Member in the market of which serious prejudice is alleged to have arisen shall, subject to the provisions of paragraph 3 of Annex V, make available to the parties to a dispute arising under Article 7, and to the panel established pursuant to paragraph 4 of Article 7, all relevant information that can be obtained as to the changes in market shares of the parties to the dispute as well as concerning prices of the products involved. — *submission and circulation of relevant information*

Article 7
Remedies

...

7.2   A request for consultations under paragraph 1 shall include a statement of available evidence with regard to *(a)* the existence and nature of the subsidy in question, and *(b)* the injury caused to the domestic industry, or the nullification or impairment, or serious prejudice[6] caused to the interests of the Member requesting consultations. — *request for consultation*

7.3   Upon request for consultations under paragraph 1, the Member believed to be granting or maintaining the subsidy practice in question shall enter into such consultations as quickly as possible. The purpose of the consultations shall be to clarify the facts of the situation and to arrive at a mutually agreed solution. — *obligation to enter into consultation*

7.4   If consultations do not result in a mutually agreed solution within 60 days[7], any Member party to such consultations may refer the matter to the DSB for the establishment of a panel, unless — *referral to DSB for establishment of a panel*

---

[6]   In the event that the request relates to a subsidy deemed to result in serious prejudice in terms of paragraph 1 of Article 6, the available evidence of serious prejudice may be limited to the available evidence as to whether the conditions of paragraph 1 of Article 6 have been met or not.

[7]   Any time-periods mentioned in this Article may be extended by mutual agreement.

the DSB decides by consensus not to establish a panel. The composition of the panel and its terms of reference shall be established within 15 days from the date when it is established.

submission and circulation of panel report

7.5   The panel shall review the matter and shall submit its final report to the parties to the dispute. The report shall be circulated to all Members within 120 days of the date of the composition and establishment of the panel's terms of reference.

See also the Decision on Part V of SCM at p. 63.

adoption of report

7.6   Within 30 days of the issuance of the panel's report to all Members, the report shall be adopted by the DSB[8,9] unless one of the parties to the dispute formally notifies the DSB of its decision to appeal or the DSB decides by consensus not to adopt the report.

appeal

7.7   Where a panel report is appealed, the Appellate Body shall issue its decision within 60 days from the date when the party to the dispute formally notifies its intention to appeal. When the Appellate Body considers that it cannot provide its report within 60 days, it shall inform the DSB in writing of the reasons for the delay together with an estimate of the period within which it will submit its report. In no case shall the proceedings exceed 90 days. The appellate report shall be adopted by the DSB and unconditionally accepted by the parties to the dispute unless the DSB decides by consensus not to adopt the appellate report within 20 days following its issuance to the Members.[8,9]

removal of adverse effects or withdrawal of subsidy

7.8   Where a panel report or an Appellate Body report is adopted in which it is determined that any subsidy has resulted in adverse effects to the interests of another Member within the meaning of Article 5, the Member granting or maintaining such subsidy shall take appropriate steps to remove the adverse effects or shall withdraw the subsidy.

countermeasures

7.9   In the event the Member has not taken appropriate steps to remove the adverse effects of the subsidy or withdraw the subsidy within six months from the date when the DSB adopts the panel report or the Appellate Body report, and in the absence of agreement on compensation, the DSB shall grant authorization to the complaining Member to take countermeasures, commensurate with the degree and nature of the adverse effects determined to exist, unless the DSB decides by consensus to reject the request.

arbitration

7.10 In the event that a party to the dispute requests arbitration under paragraph 6 of Article 22 of the DSU, the arbitrator shall

---

[8,9]   If a meeting of the DSB is not scheduled during this period, such a meeting shall be held for this purpose.

determine whether the countermeasures are commensurate with the degree and nature of the adverse effects determined to exist.

PART IV: NON-ACTIONABLE SUBSIDIES

Article 8

Identification of Non-Actionable Subsidies

...

8.5 Upon the request of a Member, the determination by the Committee referred to in paragraph 4, or a failure by the Committee to make such a determination, as well as the violation, in individual cases, of the conditions set out in a notified programme, shall be submitted to binding arbitration. The arbitration body shall present its conclusions to the Members within 120 days from the date when the matter was referred to the arbitration body. Except as otherwise provided in this paragraph, the DSU shall apply to arbitrations conducted under this paragraph.

binding arbitration after committee's determination or failture to make a determination

PART V: COUNTERVAILING MEASURES

Article 10

Application of Article VI of GATT 1994

Footnote 35

The provisions of Part II or III may be invoked in parallel with the provisions of Part V; however, with regard to the effects of a particular subsidy in the domestic market of the importing Member, only one form of relief (either a countervailing duty, if the requirements of Part V are met, or a countermeasure under Articles 4 or 7) shall be available. The provisions of Parts III and V shall not be invoked regarding measures considered non-actionable in accordance with the provisions of Part IV. However, measures referred to in paragraph 1(a) of Article 8 may be investigated in order to determine whether or not they are specific within the meaning of Article 2. In addition, in the case of a subsidy referred to in paragraph 2 of Article 8 conferred pursuant to a programme which has not been notified in accordance with paragraph 3 of Article 8, the provisions of Part III or V may be invoked, but such subsidy shall be treated as non-actionable if it is found to conform to the standards set forth in paragraph 2 of Article 8.

parallel use of Parts II or III and V, but only one form of relief permitted

investigation of non-notified measures referred to in Article 8.1(a) is permitted to determine whether subsidy is non-actionable

PART VI: INSTITUTIONS

Article 24

Committee on Subsidies and Countervailing Measures and Subsidiary Bodies

...

advisory opinions of PGE

24.4 The PGE may be consulted by any Member and may give advisory opinions on the nature of any subsidy proposed to be introduced or currently maintained by that Member. Such advisory opinions will be confidential and may not be invoked in proceedings under Article 7.

PART VIII: DEVELOPING COUNTRY MEMBERS

Article 27

Special and Differential Treatment of Developing Country Members

...

export subsidies by developing countries

27.7 The provisions of Article 4 shall not apply to a developing country Member in the case of export subsidies which are in conformity with the provisions of paragraphs 2 through 5. The relevant provisions in such a case shall be those of Article 7.

ANNEX V

PROCEDURES FOR DEVELOPING INFORMATION CONCERNING SERIOUS PREJUDICE

Members' cooperation

notification of responsible organization

1. Every Member shall cooperate in the development of evidence to be examined by a panel in procedures under paragraphs 4 through 6 of Article 7. The parties to the dispute and any third-country Member concerned shall notify to the DSB, as soon as the provisions of paragraph 4 of Article 7 have been invoked, the organization responsible for administration of this provision within its territory and the procedures to be used to comply with requests for information.

evidence

2. In cases where matters are referred to the DSB under paragraph 4 of Article 7, the DSB shall, upon request, initiate the

procedure to obtain such information from the government of the subsidizing Member as necessary to establish the existence and amount of subsidization, the value of total sales of the subsidized firms, as well as information necessary to analyze the adverse effects caused by the subsidized product.[10] This process may include, where appropriate, presentation of questions to the government of the subsidizing Member and of the complaining Member to collect information, as well as to clarify and obtain elaboration of information available to the parties to a dispute through the notification procedures set forth in Part VII.[11]

3. In the case of effects in third-country markets, a party to a dispute may collect information, including through the use of questions to the government of the third-country Member, necessary to analyse adverse effects, which is not otherwise reasonably available from the complaining Member or the subsidizing Member. This requirement should be administered in such a way as not to impose an unreasonable burden on the third-country Member. In particular, such a Member is not expected to make a market or price analysis specially for that purpose. The information to be supplied is that which is already available or can be readily obtained by this Member (e.g. most recent statistics which have already been gathered by relevant statistical services but which have not yet been published, customs data concerning imports and declared values of the products concerned, etc.). However, if a party to a dispute undertakes a detailed market analysis at its own expense, the task of the person or firm conducting such an analysis shall be facilitated by the authorities of the third-country Member and such a person or firm shall be given access to all information which is not normally maintained confidential by the government.

effects in third-country markets

4. The DSB shall designate a representative to serve the function of facilitating the information-gathering process. The sole purpose of the representative shall be to ensure the timely development of the information necessary to facilitate expeditious subsequent multilateral review of the dispute. In particular, the representative may suggest ways to most efficiently solicit necessary information as well as encourage the cooperation of the parties.

DSB representative

[10] In cases where the existence of serious prejudice has to be demonstrated.

[11] The information-gathering process by the DSB shall take into account the need to protect information which is by nature confidential or which is provided on a confidential basis by any Member involved in this process.

information-gathering process

5.   The information-gathering process outlined in paragraphs 2 through 4 shall be completed within 60 days of the date on which the matter has been referred to the DSB under paragraph 4 of Article 7. The information obtained during this process shall be submitted to the panel established by the DSB in accordance with the provisions of Part X. This information should include, *inter alia*, data concerning the amount of the subsidy in question (and, where appropriate, the value of total sales of the subsidized firms), prices of the subsidized product, prices of the non-subsidized product, prices of other suppliers to the market, changes in the supply of the subsidized product to the market in question and changes in market shares. It should also include rebuttal evidence, as well as such supplemental information as the panel deems relevant in the course of reaching its conclusions.

best information otherwise available

6.   If the subsidizing and/or third-country Member fail to cooperate in the information-gathering process, the complaining Member will present its case of serious prejudice, based on evidence available to it, together with facts and circumstances of the non-cooperation of the subsidizing and/or third-country Member. Where information is unavailable due to non-cooperation by the subsidizing and/or third-country Member, the panel may complete the record as necessary relying on best information otherwise available.

adverse inferences

7.   In making its determination, the panel should draw adverse inferences from instances of non-cooperation by any party involved in the information-gathering process.

DSB representative's advice on best information available/adverse inferences

8.   In making a determination to use either best information available or adverse inferences, the panel shall consider the advice of the DSB representative nominated under paragraph 4 as to the reasonableness of any requests for information and the efforts made by parties to comply with these requests in a cooperative and timely manner.

additional information

9.   Nothing in the information-gathering process shall limit the ability of the panel to seek such additional information it deems essential to a proper resolution to the dispute, and which was not adequately sought or developed during that process. However, ordinarily the panel should not request additional information to complete the record where the information would support a particular party's position and the absence of that information in the record is the result of unreasonable non-cooperation by that party in the information-gathering process.

DECLARATION ON DISPUTE SETTLEMENT PURSUANT TO THE AGREEMENT ON IMPLEMENTATION OF ARTICLE VI OF THE GENERAL AGREEMENT ON TARIFFS AND TRADE 1994 OR PART V OF THE AGREEMENT ON SUBSIDIES AND COUNTERVAILING MEASURES

Ministers recognize, with respect to dispute settlement pursuant to the Agreement on Implementation of Article VI of GATT 1994 or Part V of the Agreement on Subsidies and Countervailing Measures, the need for the consistent resolution of disputes arising from anti-dumping and countervailing duty measures.

consistent resolution of dispute arising from anti-dumping and countervailing measures

ANNEX 1B
GENERAL AGREEMENT ON TRADE IN SERVICES

Article XXI
Modification of Schedules

...

arbitration

3. (a) If agreement is not reached between the modifying Member and any affected Member before the end of the period provided for negotiations, such affected Member may refer the matter to arbitration. Any affected Member that wishes to enforce a right that it may have to compensation must participate in the arbitration.

(b) If no affected Member has requested arbitration, the modifying Member shall be free to implement the proposed modification or withdrawal.

implementation of such arbitration

4. (a) The modifying Member may not modify or withdraw its commitment until it has made compensatory adjustments in conformity with the findings of the arbitration.

(b) If the modifying Member implements its proposed modification or withdrawal and does not comply with the findings of the arbitration, any affected Member that participated in the arbitration may modify or withdraw substantially equivalent benefits in conformity with those findings. Notwithstanding Article II, such a modification or withdrawal may be implemented solely with respect to the modifying Member.

PART V
INSTITUTIONAL PROVISIONS

Article XXII
Consultation

DSU applies to consultations

1. Each Member shall accord sympathetic consideration to, and shall afford adequate opportunity for, consultation regarding such representations as may be made by any other Member with respect to any matter affecting the operation of this Agreement. The Dispute Settlement Understanding (DSU) shall apply to such consultations.

consultations with Members by the CTS or by DSB

2. The Council for Trade in Services or the Dispute Settlement Body (DSB) may, at the request of a Member, consult with any Member or Members in respect of any matter for which it has not been

possible to find a satisfactory solution through consultation under paragraph 1.

3. A Member may not invoke Article XVII, either under this Article or Article XXIII, with respect to a measure of another Member that falls within the scope of an international agreement between them relating to the avoidance of double taxation. In case of disagreement between Members as to whether a measure falls within the scope of such an agreement between them, it shall be open to either Member to bring this matter before the Council for Trade in Services.[1] The Council shall refer the matter to arbitration. The decision of the arbitrator shall be final and binding on the Members.

double taxation issues

arbitration

Article XXIII

Dispute Settlement and Enforcement

1. If any Member should consider that any other Member fails to carry out its obligations or specific commitments under this Agreement, it may with a view to reaching a mutually satisfactory resolution of the matter have recourse to the DSU.

recourse to the DSU

2. If the DSB considers that the circumstances are serious enough to justify such action, it may authorize a Member or Members to suspend the application to any other Member or Members of obligations and specific commitments in accordance with Article 22 of the DSU.

suspension of obligations

3. If any Member considers that any benefit it could reasonably have expected to accrue to it under a specific commitment of another Member under Part III of this Agreement is being nullified or impaired as a result of the application of any measure which does not conflict with the provisions of this Agreement, it may have recourse to the DSU. If the measure is determined by the DSB to have nullified or impaired such a benefit, the Member affected shall be entitled to a mutually satisfactory adjustment on the basis of paragraph 2 of Article XXI, which may include the modification or withdrawal of the measure. In the event an agreement cannot be reached between the Members concerned, Article 22 of the DSU shall apply.

violation, nullification and impairment

---

[1] With respect to agreements on the avoidance of double taxation which exist on the date of entry into force of the WTO Agreement, such a matter may be brought before the Council for Trade in Services only with the consent of both parties to such an agreement.

ANNEX 1B
GENERAL AGREEMENT ON TRADE IN SERVICES

ANNEX ON FINANCIAL SERVICES

...

4.   Dispute Settlement

panel expertise   Panels for disputes on prudential issues and other financial matters shall have the necessary expertise relevant to the specific financial service under dispute.

See DSU 8 at p. 9.

ANNEX ON AIR TRANSPORT SERVICES

...

exhaustion of other procedures   4.   The dispute settlement procedures of the Agreement may be invoked only where obligations or specific commitments have been assumed by the concerned Members and where dispute settlement procedures in bilateral and other multilateral agreements or arrangements have been exhausted.

DECISION ON CERTAIN DISPUTE SETTLEMENT PROCEDURES FOR THE GENERAL AGREEMENT ON TRADE IN SERVICES

...

1.   A roster of panelists shall be established to assist in the selection of panelists.

roster

2.   To this end, Members may suggest names of individuals possessing the qualifications referred to in paragraph 3 for inclusion on the roster, and shall provide a curriculum vitae of their qualifications including, if applicable, indication of sector-specific expertise.

nominations

3.   Panels shall be composed of well-qualified governmental and/or non-governmental individuals who have experience in issues related to the General Agreement on Trade in Services and/or trade in services, including associated regulatory matters. Panelists shall serve in their individual capacities and not as representatives of any government or organisation.

qualifications

4.   Panels for disputes regarding sectoral matters shall have the necessary expertise relevant to the specific services sectors which the dispute concerns.

sectoral expertise

5.   The Secretariat shall maintain the roster and shall develop procedures for its administration in consultation with the Chairman of the Council.

maintenance of roster

See DSU 8.4 at p. 10.

ANNEX IC
AGREEMENT OF TRADE-RELATED ASPECTS OF
INTELLECTUAL PROPERTY RIGHTS

Article 64

Dispute Settlement

1.　The provisions of Articles XXII and XXIII of GATT 1994 as elaborated and applied by the Dispute Settlement Understanding shall apply to consultations and the settlement of disputes under this Agreement except as otherwise specifically provided herein.

2.　Subparagraphs 1(b) and 1(c) of Article XXIII of GATT 1994 shall not apply to the settlement of disputes under this Agreement for a period of five years from the date of entry into force of the WTO Agreement.

3.　During the time period referred to in paragraph 2, the Council for TRIPS shall examine the scope and modalities for complaints of the type provided for under subparagraphs 1(b) and 1(c) of Article XXIII of GATT 1994 made pursuant to this Agreement, and submit its recommendations to the Ministerial Conference for approval. Any decision of the Ministerial Conference to approve such recommendations or to extend the period in paragraph 2 shall be made only by consensus, and approved recommendations shall be effective for all Members without further formal acceptance process.

DECISION OF 12 APRIL 1989 ON IMPROVEMENTS TO THE GATT DISPUTE SETTLEMENT RULES AND PROCEDURES

*[Montreal Decision referred to in DSU 26.2 at p. 31,
applicable to situation complaints under
GATT 1994 XXIII(1)(c), BISD 36S/61]*

...

G. Adoption of Panel Reports

1. In order to provide sufficient time for the members of the Council to consider panel reports, the reports shall not be considered for adoption by the Council until thirty days after they have been issued to the contracting parties. *minimum time period prior to consideration for adoption*

2. Contracting parties having objections to panel reports shall give written reasons to explain their objections for circulation at least ten days prior to the Council meeting at which the panel report will be considered. *objections*

3. The parties to a dispute shall have the right to participate fully in the consideration of the panel report by the Council, and their views shall be fully recorded. The practice of adopting panel reports by consensus shall be continued, without prejudice to the GATT provisions on decision-making which remain applicable. However, the delaying of the process of dispute settlement shall be avoided. *participation of parties* *consensus*

4. The period from the request under Article XXII:1 or Article XXIII:1 until the Council takes a decision on the panel report shall not, unless agreed to by the parties, exceed fifteen months. The provisions of this paragraph shall not affect the provisions of paragraph 6 of Section F(f). *duration of process until decision on panel report*

I. Surveillance of Implementation of Recommendations and Rulings

1. Prompt compliance with recommendations or rulings of the CONTRACTING PARTIES under Article XXIII is essential in order to ensure effective resolution of disputes to the benefit of all contracting parties. *prompt compliance*

2. The contracting party concerned shall inform the Council of its intentions in respect of implementation of the recommendations or rulings. If it is impracticable to comply immediately with the recommendations or rulings, the contracting party concerned shall have a reasonable period of time in which to do so. *information on implementation*

monitoring of
implementation

3.   The Council shall monitor the implementation of recommendations or rulings adopted under Article XXIII:2. The issue of implementation of the recommendations or rulings may be raised at the Council by any contracting party at any time following their adoption. Unless the Council decides otherwise, the issue of implementation of the recommendations or rulings shall be on the agenda of the Council meeting after six months following their adoption and shall remain on the Council's agenda until the issue is resolved. At least ten days prior to each such Council meeting, the contracting party concerned shall provide the Council with a status report in writing of its progress in the implementation of the panel recommendations or rulings.

developing
countries

4.   In cases brought by developing contracting parties, the Council shall consider what further action it might take which would be appropriate to the circumstances, in conformity with paragraphs 21 and 23 of the 1979 Understanding regarding Notification, Consultation, Dispute Settlement and Surveillance (BISD 26S/214).

[The 1979 Understanding Regarding Notification, Consultation, Dispute Settlement and Surveillance is not reproduced in this volume but can be found in BISD 26S/214.]

PROCEDURES UNDER ARTICLE XXIII
Decision of 5 April 1966

[Applicable to procedures with Developing Countries. See DSU 3.12 at p. 5.]

The CONTRACTING PARTIES,

Recognizing that the prompt settlement of situations in which a contracting party considers that any benefits accruing to it directly or indirectly from the General Agreement are being impaired by measures taken by another contracting party, is essential to the effective functioning of the General Agreement and the maintenance of a proper balance between the rights and obligations of all contracting parties;

Recognizing further that the existence of such a situation can cause severe damage to the trade and economic development of the less-developed contracting parties; and

Affirming their resolve to facilitate the solution of such situations while taking fully into account the need for safeguarding both the present and potential trade of less-developed contracting parties affected by such measures;

Decide that:

1.   If consultations between a less-developed contracting party and a developed contracting party in regard to any matter falling under paragraph 1 of Article XXIII do not lead to a satisfactory settlement, the less-developed contracting party complaining of the measure may refer the matter which is the subject of consultations to the Director-General so that, acting in an *ex officio* capacity, he may use his good offices with a view to facilitating a solution,.   *good offices of DG*

2.   To this effect the contracting parties concerned shall, at the request of the Director-General, promptly furnish all relevant information.   *relevant information*

3.   On receipt of this information, the Director-General shall consult with the contracting parties concerned and with such other contracting parties or inter-governmental organizations as he considers appropriate with a view to promoting a mutually acceptable solution.   *consultations of DG*

4.   After a period of two months from the commencement of the consultations referred to in paragraph 3 above, if no mutually

referral to CPs

satisfactory solution has been reached, the Director-General shall, at the request of one of the contracting parties concerned, bring the matter to the attention of the CONTRACTING PARTIES or the Council, to whom he shall submit a report on the action taken by him, together with all background information.

establishment of panel

5.   Upon receipt of the report, the CONTRACTING PARTIES or the Council shall forthwith appoint a panel of experts to examine the matter with a view to recommending appropriate solutions. The members of the panel shall act a personal capacity and shall be appointed in consultation with, and with the approval of, the contracting parties concerned.

examination by panel

6.   In conducting its examination and having before it all the background information, the panel shall take due account of all the circumstances and considerations relating to the application of the measures complained of, and their impact on the trade and economic development of affected contracting parties.

panel report

non-violation

7.   The panel shall, within a period of sixty days from the date the matter was referred to it, submit its findings and recommendations to the CONTRACTING PARTIES or to the Council, for consideration and decision. Where the matter is referred to the Council, it may, in accordance with Rule 8 of the Intersessional Procedures adopted by the CONTRACTING PARTIES at their thirteenth session[1], address its recommendations directly to the interested contracting parties and concurrently report to the CONTRACTING PARTIES.

report on action taken

8.   Within a period of ninety days from the date of the decision of the CONTRACTING PARTIES or the Council, the contracting party to which a recommendation is directed shall report to the CONTRACTING PARTIES or the Council on the action taken by it in pursuance of the decision.

authorization to suspend application of obligations

9.   If on examination of this report it is found that a contracting party to which a recommendation has been directed has not complied in full with the relevant recommendation of the CONTRACTING PARTIES or the Council, and that any benefit accruing directly or indirectly under the General Agreement continued in consequence to be nullified or impaired, and that the circumstances are serious enough to justify such action, the CONTRACTING PARTIES may authorize the affected contracting party or

---

[1]   BISD, Seventh Supplement, page 7.

parties to suspend, in regard to the contracting party causing the damage, application of any concession or any other obligation under the General Agreement whose suspension is considered warranted, taking account of the circumstances.

10.   In the event that a recommendation to a developed country by the CONTRACTING PARTIES is not applied within the time-limit prescribed in paragraph 8, the CONTRACTING PARTIES shall consider what measures, further to those undertaken under paragraph 9, should be taken to resolve the matter.

further action

11.   If consultations, held under paragraph 2 of Article XXXVII, relate to restrictions for which there is no authority under any provisions of the General Agreement, any of the parties to the consultations may, in the absence of a satisfactory solution, request that consultations be carried out by the CONTRACTING PARTIES pursuant to paragraph 2 of Article XXIII and in accordance with the procedures set out in the present decision, it being understood that a consultation held under paragraph 2 of Article XXXVII in respect of such restrictions will be considered by the CONTRACTING PARTIES as fulfilling the conditions of paragraph 1 of Article XXIII if the parties to the consultations so agree.

consultations under Article XXXVII:2

consultations under Article XXIII:2

TRANSITIONAL CO-EXISTENCE OF THE GATT 1947 AND THE WTO AGREEMENT

Decision of 8 December 1994 adopted by the Preparatory Committee for the WTO and the CONTRACTING PARTIES to GATT 1947

The PREPARATORY COMMITTEE FOR THE WORLD TRADE ORGANIZATION

invites the CONTRACTING PARTIES to the General Agreement on Tariffs and Trade 1947 to take the following decision:

The CONTRACTING PARTIES to the General Agreement on Tariffs and Trade (hereinafter referred to as "GATT 1947"),

Noting that not all contracting parties to the GATT 1947 meeting the conditions for original membership in the World Trade Organization (hereinafter referred "WTO") will be able to accept the Marrakesh Agreement Establishing the WTO (hereinafter referred to as "WTO Agreement") as of its date of entry into force, and that the stability of multilateral trade relations would therefore be furthered if the GATT 1947 and the WTO Agreement were to co-exist for a limited period of time;

Considering that, during that period of co-existence, a contracting party which has become a Member of the WTO should not be under a legal obligation to extend the benefits accruing solely under the WTO Agreement to contracting parties that have not yet become WTO Members and should have the right to act in accordance with the WTO Agreement notwithstanding its obligations under the GATT 1947;

Desiring to end the period of co-existence on a date agreed in advance so as to provide predictability for policy makers and facilitate an orderly termination of the institutional framework of the GATT 1947;

Decide as follows:

priority of WTO provisions

1. The contracting parties that are Members of the WTO may, notwithstanding the provisions of the GATT 1947,

   (a) accord to products originating in or destined for a Member of the WTO the benefits to be accorded to such products solely as a result of concessions, commitments or other obligations assumed under the WTO Agreement without according such benefits to products originating in or destined for a contracting party that has not yet become a Member of the WTO; and

benefits under WTO agreement

(b)   maintain or adopt any measure consistent with the provisions of the WTO Agreement.

measures consistent with WTO Agreement

2.   The provisions of Article XXIII of the GATT 1947 shall not apply:

(a)   to disputes brought against a contracting party which is a Member of the WTO if the dispute concerns a measure that is identified as a specific measure at issue in a request for the establishment of a panel made in accordance with Article 6 of the Understanding on Rules and Procedures Governing the Settlement of Disputes in Annex 2 of the WTO Agreement and the dispute settlement proceedings following that request are being pursued or are completed; and

priority of WTO dispute settlement procedure

(b)   in respect of measures covered by paragraph 1 above.

3.   The legal instruments through which the contracting parties apply the GATT 1947 are herewith terminated one year after the date of entry into force of the WTO Agreement. In the light of unforeseen circumstances, the CONTRACTING PARTIES may decide to postpone the date of termination by no more than one year.

termination of application of GATT 1947

TRANSITIONAL ARRANGEMENTS

AVOIDANCE OF PROCEDURAL AND INSTITUTIONAL DUPLICATION

Decision of 8 December 1994 adopted by the Preparatory Committee for the WTO and the CONTRACTING PARTIES to GATT 1947

The PREPARATORY COMMITTEE FOR THE WORLD TRADE ORGANIZATION

Noting that the General Agreement on Tariffs and Trade (hereinafter referred to as "GATT 1947") and the Marrakesh Agreement Establishing the World Trade Organization (hereinafter referred to as "WTO Agreement") are legally distinct and that Members of the WTO may therefore remain contracting parties to the GATT 1947;

Considering that contracting parties to the GATT 1947 and parties to the Tokyo Round Agreements that are also Members of the WTO should not be subjected to the inconvenience of having to notify and consult on their measures and policies twice;

Desiring, therefore, that the bodies established under the GATT 1947, the Tokyo Round Agreements and the WTO Agreement coordinate their activities to the extent that their functions overlap;

Decides to propose the following procedures for adoption by the CONTRACTING PARTIES to the GATT 1947, the Committees established under the Tokyo Round Agreements and the General Council of the WTO:

In the period between the date of entry into force of the WTO Agreement and the date of the termination of the legal instruments through which the contracting parties apply the GATT 1947 and of the Tokyo Round Agreements the following notification and coordination procedures shall apply under the GATT 1947, the Tokyo Round Agreements and the WTO Agreement:

notification procedures

1.   If a measure is subject to a notification obligation both under the WTO Agreement and under the GATT 1947 or a Tokyo Round Agreement, the notification of such a measure to a WTO body shall, unless otherwise indicated in the notification, be deemed to be also a notification of that measure under the GATT 1947 or the Tokyo Round Agreement. Any such notification shall

be circulated by the WTO Secretariat simultaneously to the Members of the WTO and to the contracting parties to the GATT 1947 and/or the parties to the Tokyo Round Agreement. These procedures are without prejudice to any notification procedures applicable in specific areas.

2.   The coordination procedures set out in paragraphs 3 and 4 below shall apply in the relations between the bodies referred to in sub-paragraphs (a) to (d) below:

bodies

(a)   The following Committees established under the GATT 1947 or a Tokyo Round Agreement shall coordinate their activities with the corresponding Committees established under the WTO Agreement:

scope of coordination procedures

Committee on Trade and Development,

Committee on Balance-of-Payments Restrictions,

Committee on Anti-Dumping Practices,

Committee on Customs Valuation,

Committee on Import Licensing,

Committee on Subsidies and Countervailing Measures,

Committee on Technical Barriers to Trade.

(b)   The Committee on Tariff Concessions and the Technical Group on Quantitative Restrictions and Other Non-Tariff Measures of the GATT 1947 shall coordinate their activities with the WTO Committee on Market Access proposed to be established.

(c)   The Working Parties established under the GATT 1947 to examine a regional agreement or arrangement shall coordinate their activities with Working Parties of the WTO that examine the same regional agreement or arrangement.[1]

(d)   The GATT 1947 Council of Representatives shall coordinate its trade policy reviews with those of the WTO Trade Policy Review Body.

---

[1]   The Working Parties of the WTO include Working Parties originating from decisions of the CONTRACTING PARTIES to the GATT 1947 that were adopted before the entry into force of the WTO Agreement and therefore form part of the GATT 1994.

coordination
procedures

3.   The bodies established under the GATT 1947 or a Tokyo Round Agreement that are referred to in paragraph 2 above shall hold their meetings jointly or consecutively, as appropriate, with the corresponding WTO bodies. In meetings held jointly the rules of procedure to be applied by the WTO body shall be followed. The reports on joint meetings shall be submitted to the competent bodies established under the GATT 1947, the Tokyo Round Agreements and the WTO Agreement.

respect of existing
rights and
obligations

4.   The coordination of activities in accordance with paragraph 3 above shall be conducted in a manner which ensures that the enjoyment of the rights and the performance of the obligations under the GATT 1947, the Tokyo Round Agreements and the WTO Agreement and the exercise of the competence of the CONTRACTING PARTIES to the GATT 1947, the Committees established under the Tokyo Round Agreements and the bodies of the WTO are unaffected.

termination

5.   The CONTRACTING PARTIES to the GATT 1947, the Committees established under the Tokyo Round Agreements and the General Council of the WTO may decide independently to terminate the application of the provisions set out in paragraphs 1 to 4 above.

COMMITTEE ON ANTI-DUMPING PRACTICES

TRANSITIONAL CO-EXISTENCE OF THE AGREEMENT ON IMPLEMENTATION OF ARTICLE VI OF THE GENERAL AGREEMENT ON TARIFFS AND TRADE AND THE MARRAKESH AGREEMENT ESTABLISHING THE WORLD TRADE ORGANIZATION

Decision adopted by the Committee on 8 December 1994 at the Invitation of the Preparatory Committee for the World Trade Organization

The Parties to the Agreement on Implementation of Article VI of the General Agreement on Tariffs and Trade (hereinafter referred to as "the Agreement"),

Noting that not all Parties to the Agreement meeting the conditions for original membership in the World Trade Organization (hereinafter referred to as the "WTO") will be able to accept the Marrakesh Agreement Establishing the WTO (hereinafter referred to as the "WTO Agreement") as of its date of entry into force, and that the stability of multilateral trade relations would therefore be furthered if the Agreement and the WTO Agreement were to co-exist for a limited period of time;

Considering that, during that period of co-existence, a Party to the Agreement which has become a Member of the WTO should have the right to act in accordance with the WTO Agreement notwithstanding its obligations under the Agreement;

Desiring to end the period of co-existence on a date agreed in advance so as to provide predictability for policy makers and facilitate an orderly termination of the institutional framework of the Agreement;

Decide as follows:

1. The Parties to the Agreement that are Members of the WTO may, notwithstanding the provisions of the Agreement, maintain or adopt any measure consistent with the provisions of the WTO Agreement.

measures consistent with WTO Agreement

2.   The dispute settlement provisions of the Agreement shall not apply:

priority of WTO dispute settlement procedure

(a)   to disputes brought against a Party to the Agreement which is a Member of the WTO if the dispute concerns a measure that is identified as a specific measure at issue in the request for the establishment of a panel made in accordance with Article 6 of the Understanding on Rules and Procedures Governing the Settlement of Disputes in Annex 2 of the WTO Agreement and the dispute settlement proceedings following that request are being pursued or are completed; and

(b)   in respect of measures covered by paragraph 1 above.

termination of Agreement

3.   The Agreement is herewith terminated one year after the date of entry into force of the WTO Agreement. In the light of unforeseen circumstances, the Parties may decide to postpone the date of termination by no more than one year.

COMMITTEE ON ANTI-DUMPING PRACTICES

CONSEQUENCES OF WITHDRAWAL FROM
OR TERMINATION OF THE AGREEMENT ON
IMPLEMENTATION OF ARTICLE VI OF THE
GENERAL AGREEMENT ON TARIFFS
AND TRADE

*Decision adopted by the Committee on 8 December 1994
at the Invitation of the Preparatory Committee of the
World Trade Organization*

*[Because of the special nature and duration of Anti-Dumping
investigations specific decisions were adopted extending
the possible effect of the Anti-Dumping Code
to a period up to two years]*

The Parties to the Agreement on Implementation of Article VI of the General Agreement on Tariffs and Trade (hereinafter "the Agreement"),

Recalling the Ministerial Decision of 15 April 1994 on the Application and Review of the Understanding on Rules and Procedures Governing the Settlement of Disputes,

Further recalling that Parties to the Agreement have the right to withdraw from the Agreement at any time, said withdrawal to take effect upon the expiration of sixty days from the day on which written notice is received by the Director-General to the CONTRACTING PARTIES to GATT 1947;

Agree that, in the event of withdrawal by any Party from the Agreement taking effect on or after the date of entry into force for it of the Marrakesh Agreement Establishing the World Trade Organization (hereinafter "WTO Agreement"), or in case of termination of the Agreement while this Decision is in effect: *withdrawal from or termination of Agreement*

(a) the Agreement shall continue to apply with respect to any anti-dumping investigation or review which is not subject to application of the Agreement on Implementation of Article VI of the General Agreement on Tariffs and Trade 1994 pursuant to the terms of Article 18:3 of that Agreement. *continued application of the Agreement*

(b) Parties that withdraw from the Agreement shall remain Members of the Committee on Anti-Dumping Practices exclusively for the purpose of dealing with any *continued Committee membership*

dispute arising out of any anti-dumping investigation or review identified in paragraph (a).

continued   (c)   In case of termination of the Agreement during the
operation of   period of validity of this Decision the Committee on
Committee   Anti-Dumping Practices shall remain in operation for the purpose of dealing with any dispute arising out of any anti-dumping investigation or review identified in paragraph (a).

applicable rules   (d)   The rules and procedures for the settlement of disputes
and procedures   arising under the Agreement applicable immediately prior to the date of entry into force of the WTO Agreement shall apply to disputes arising out of any investigation or review identified in paragraph (a). With respect to such disputes for which consultations are requested after the date of this Decision, Parties and panels will be guided by Article 19 of the Understanding on Rules and Procedures Governing the Settlement of Disputes in Annex 2 of the WTO Agreement.

best efforts to   (e)   Parties will make their best efforts to expedite to the
expedite   extent possible under their domestic legislation inves-
investigations   tigations and reviews referred to in paragraph (a), and to
and reviews   expedite procedures for the settlement of disputes so as to permit Committee consideration of such disputes within the period of validity of this Decision.

validity of decision   This Decision shall remain in effect for a period of two years after the date of entry into force of the WTO Agreement. Any Party to the Agreement as of the date of this Decision may renounce this Decision. The renunciation shall take effect upon

renunciation   the expiration of sixty days from the day on which written notice
of decision   of renunciation is received by the person who performs the depository function of the Director-General to the CONTRACTING PARTIES to GATT 1947.

COMMITTEE ON SUBSIDIES AND COUNTERVAILING MEASURES

TRANSITIONAL CO-EXISTENCE OF THE AGREEMENT ON INTERPRETATION AND APPLICATION OF ARTICLES VI, XVI AND XXIII OF THE GENERAL AGREEMENT ON TARIFFS AND TRADE AND THE MARRAKESH AGREEMENT ESTABLISHING THE WORLD TRADE ORGANIZATION

*Decision adopted by the Committee on 8 December 1994
at the Invitation of the Preparatory Committee for the
World Trade Organization*

The signatories to the Agreement on Interpretation and Application of Articles VI, XVI and XXIII of the General Agreement on Tariffs and Trade (hereinafter referred to as "the Agreement"),

Noting that not all signatories to the Agreement meeting the conditions for original membership in the World Trade Organization (hereinafter referred to as the "WTO") will be able to accept the Marrakesh Agreement Establishing the WTO (hereinafter referred to as the "WTO Agreement") as of its date of entry into force, and that the stability of multilateral trade relations would therefore be furthered if the Agreement and the WTO Agreement were to co-exist for a limited period of time;

Considering that, during that period of co-existence, a signatory to the Agreement which has become a Member of the WTO should have the right to act in accordance with the WTO Agreement notwithstanding its obligations under the Agreement;

Desiring to end the period of co-existence on a date agreed in advance so as to provide predictability for policy makers and facilitate an orderly termination of the institutional framework of the Agreement;

Decide as follows:

1.   The signatories to the Agreement that are Members of the WTO may, notwithstanding the provisions of the Agreement, maintain or adopt any measure consistent with the provisions of the WTO Agreement.

*measures
consistent with
WTO Agreement*

2. The dispute settlement provisions of the Agreement shall not apply:

priority of WTO
dispute settlement
procedure

(a) to disputes brought against a signatory to the Agreement which is a Member of the WTO if the dispute concerns a measure that is identified as a specific measure at issue in the request for the establishment of a panel made in accordance with Article 6 of the Understanding on Rules and Procedures Governing the Settlement of Disputes in Annex 2 of the WTO Agreement and the dispute settlement proceedings following that request are being pursued or are completed; and

(b) in respect of measures covered by paragraph 1 above.

termination
of Agreement

3. The Agreement is herewith terminated one year after the date of entry into force of the WTO Agreement. In the light of unforeseen circumstances, the signatories may decide to postpone the date of termination by no more than one year.

COMMITTEE ON SUBSIDIES AND COUNTERVAILING MEASURES

CONSEQUENCES OF WITHDRAWAL FROM OR TERMINATION OF THE AGREEMENT ON INTERPRETATION AND APPLICATION OF ARTICLES VI, XVI AND XXIII OF THE GENERAL AGREEMENT ON TARIFFS AND TRADE

Decision adopted by the Committee on 8 December 1994 at the Invitation of the Preparatory Committee of the World Trade Organization

[Because of the special nature and duration of Subsidies investigations specific decisions were adopted extending the possible effect of the Subsidies Code to a period up to two years]

The signatories to the Agreement on Interpretation and Application of Articles VI, XVI and XXIII of the General Agreement on Tariffs and Trade (hereinafter "the Agreement"),

Recalling the Ministerial Decision of 15 April 1994 on the Application and Review of the Understanding on Rules and Procedures Governing the Settlement of Disputes,

Further recalling that signatories to the Agreement have the right to withdraw from the Agreement at any time, said withdrawal to take effect upon the expiration of sixty days from the day on which written notice is received by the Director-General to the CONTRACTING PARTIES to GATT 1947;

Agree that, in the event of withdrawal by any signatory from the Agreement taking effect on or after the date of entry into force for it of the Marrakesh Agreement Establishing the World Trade Organization (hereinafter "WTO Agreement"), or in case of termination of the Agreement while this Decision is in effect: **_withdrawal from or termination of Agreement_**

(a) the Agreement shall continue to apply with respect to any countervailing duty investigation or review which is not subject to application of the WTO Agreement on Subsidies and Countervailing Measures pursuant to the terms of Article 32.3 of that Agreement. **_continued application of Agreement_**

(b) Signatories that withdraw from the Agreement shall remain Members of the Committee on Subsidies and Countervailing Measures exclusively for the purpose **_continued Committee membership_**

of dealing with any dispute arising out of any countervailing duty investigation or review identified in paragraph (a).

continued
operation of the
Committee

(c) In case of termination of the Agreement during the
period of validity of this Decision the Committee on
Subsidies and Countervailing Measures shall remain in
operation for the purpose of dealing with any dispute
arising out of any countervailing duty investigation or
review identified in paragraph (a).

applicable rules
and procedures

(d) The rules and procedures for the settlement of disputes
arising under the Agreement applicable immediately
prior to the date of entry into force of the WTO
Agreement shall apply to disputes arising out of any
investigation or review identified in paragraph (a). With
respect to such disputes for which consultations are
requested after the date of this Decision, signatories and
panels will be guided by Article 19 of the Understanding on Rules and Procedures Governing the Settlement
of Disputes in Annex 2 of the WTO Agreement.

best efforts to
expedite
investigations
and reviews

(e) Signatories will make their best efforts to expedite to the
extent possible under their domestic legislation investigations and reviews referred to in paragraph (a), and to
expedite procedures for the settlement of disputes so as
to permit Committee consideration of such disputes
within the period of validity of this Decision.

validity of decision

This Decision shall remain in effect for a period of two years
after the date of entry into force of the WTO Agreement. Any
signatory to the Agreement as of the date of this Decision may
renounce this Decision. The renunciation shall take effect

renunciation
of decision

upon the expiration of sixty days from the day on which
written notice of renunciation is received by the person who
performs the depository function of the Director-General to
the CONTRACTING PARTIES to GATT 1947.

AGREEMENT ON GOVERNMENT PROCUREMENT

Article XXII

Consultations and Dispute Settlement

1. The provisions of the Understanding on Rules and Proce- *applicability*
dures Governing the Settlement of Disputes under the WTO *of the DSU*
Agreement (hereinafter referred to as the "Dispute Settlement
Understanding") shall be applicable except as otherwise specifically provided below.

2. If any Party considers that any benefit accruing to it, directly *nullification or*
or indirectly, under this Agreement is being nullified or impaired, *impairment,*
or that the attainment of any objective of this Agreement is being *objective of the*
impeded as the result of the failure of another Party or Parties to *Agreement*
carry out its obligations under this Agreement, or the application *impeded, or non-*
by another Party or Parties of any measure, whether or not it *violation claims*
conflicts with the provisions of this Agreement, it may with a view
to reaching a mutually satisfactory resolution of the matter, make
written representations or proposals to the other Party or Parties
which it considers to be concerned. Such action shall be promptly
notified to the Dispute Settlement Body established under the
Dispute Settlement Understanding (hereinafter referred to as *sympathetic*
"DSB"), as specified below. Any Party thus approached shall give *consideration*
sympathetic consideration to the representations or proposals
made to it.

3. The DSB shall have the authority to establish panels, adopt *DSB's authority*
panel and Appellate Body reports, make recommendations or
give rulings on the matter, maintain surveillance of implementation of rulings and recommendations, and authorize suspension of
concessions and other obligations under this Agreement or con- *only Members of*
sultations regarding remedies when withdrawal of measures *this Agreement*
found to be in contravention of the Agreement is not possible, *participate in DSB*
provided that only Members of the WTO Party to this Agreement *decisions or*
shall participate in decisions or actions taken by the DSB with *actions*
respect to disputes under this Agreement.

4. Panels shall have the following terms of reference unless the
parties to the dispute agree otherwise within 20 days of the
establishment of the panel:

terms of reference

"To examine, in the light of the relevant provisions of this Agreement and of (name of any other covered Agreement cited by the parties to the dispute), the matter referred to the DSB by (name of party) in document ... and to make such findings as will assist the DSB in making the recommendations or in giving the rulings provided for in this Agreement."

if claims under various agreements

In the case of a dispute in which provisions both of this Agreement and of one or more other Agreements listed in Appendix 1 of the Dispute Settlement Understanding are invoked by one of the parties to the dispute, paragraph 3 shall apply only to those parts of the panel report concerning the interpretation and application of this Agreement.

qualified panelists

5.   Panels established by the DSB to examine disputes under this Agreement shall include persons qualified in the area of government procurement.

See also DSU 8 at p. 9-10.

duration of panel proceedings

6.   Every effort shall be made to accelerate the proceedings to the greatest extent possible. Notwithstanding the provisions of paragraphs 8 and 9 of Article 12 of the Dispute Settlement Understanding, the panel shall attempt to provide its final report to the parties to the dispute not later than four months, and in case of delay not later than seven months, after the date on which the composition and terms of reference of the panel are agreed. Consequently, every effort shall be made to reduce also the periods foreseen in paragraph 1 of Article 20 and paragraph 4 of Article 21 of the Dispute Settlement Understanding by two months. Moreover, notwithstanding the provisions of paragraph 5 of Article 21 of the Dispute Settlement Understanding, the panel shall attempt to issue its decision, in case of a disagreement as to the existence or consistency with a covered Agreement of measures taken to comply with the recommendations and rulings, within 60 days.

no cross-retaliation

7.   Notwithstanding paragraph 2 of Article 22 of the Dispute Settlement Understanding, any dispute arising under any Agreement listed in Appendix 1 to the Dispute Settlement Understanding other than this Agreement shall not result in the suspension of concessions or other obligations under this Agreement, and any dispute arising under this Agreement shall not result in the suspension of concessions or other obligations under any other Agreement listed in the said Appendix 1.

AGREEMENT ON TRADE
IN CIVIL AIRCRAFT

Article 8

Surveillance, Review, Consultation, and
Dispute Settlement

...

8.5   Each Signatory shall afford sympathetic consideration to and adequate opportunity for prompt consultation regarding representations made by another Signatory with respect to any matter affecting the operation of this Agreement.

consultations

8.6   Signatories recognize the desirability of consultations with other Signatories in the Committee in order to seek a mutually acceptable solution prior to the initiation of an investigation to determine the existence, degree and effect of any alleged subsidy. In those exceptional circumstances in which no consultations occur before such domestic procedures are initiated, Signatories shall notify the Committee immediately of initiation of such procedures and enter into simultaneous consultations to seek a mutually agreed solution that would obviate the need for countervailing measures.

notification of initiation of investigation of alleged subsidy

consultations

8.7   Should a Signatory consider that its trade interests in civil aircraft manufacture, repair, maintenance, rebuilding, modification or conversion have been or are likely to be adversely affected by any action by another Signatory, it may request review of the matter by the Committee. Upon such a request, the Committee shall convene within thirty days and shall review the matter as quickly as possible with a view to resolving the issues involved as promptly as possible and in particular prior to final resolution of these issues elsewhere. In this connection the Committee may issue such rulings or recommendations as may be appropriate. Such review shall be without prejudice to the rights of Signatories under the GATT or under instruments multilaterally negotiated under the auspices of the GATT, as they affect trade in civil aircraft. For the purposes of aiding consideration of the issues involved, under the GATT and such instruments, the Committee may provide such technical assistance as may be appropriate.

interest likely to be adversely affected

review by the Committee

rulings or recommendations

technical assistance by the Committee

8.8   Signatories agree that, with respect to any dispute related to a matter covered by this Agreement, but not covered by other instruments multilaterally negotiated under the auspices of the

dispute settlement
procedures

GATT, the provisions of Articles XXII and XXIII of the General Agreement and the provisions of the Understanding related to Notification, Consultation, Dispute Settlement and Surveillance shall be applied, mutatis mutandis, by the Signatories and the Committee for the purposes of seeking settlement of such dispute. These procedures shall also be applied for the settlement of any dispute related to a matter covered by this Agreement and by another instrument multilaterally negotiated under the auspices of the GATT, should the parties to the dispute so agree.

[The provisions of the Understanding related to Notification , Consultation, Dispute Settlement and Surveillance are not reproduced in the present volume but can be found in BISD 26S /210.]

INTERNATIONAL DAIRY AGREEMENT

Article IV

Functions of the International Dairy Council and Cooperation between the Parties

...

5.   Any Party may raise before the Council any matter[1] affecting this Agreement, *inter alia*, for the same purposes provided for in paragraph 2. Each Party shall promptly afford adequate opportunity for consultation regarding such matter affecting this Agreement.

consultations

6.   If the matter affects the application of the specific provisions of the Annex, any Party which considers that its trade interests are being seriously threatened and which is unable to reach a mutually satisfactory solution with the other Party or Parties concerned may request the Chairman of the Committee established under paragraph 2(a) of Article VII, to convene a special meeting of the Committee on an urgent basis so as to determine as rapidly as possible, and within four working days if requested, any measures which may be required to meet the situation. If a satisfactory solution cannot be reached, the Council shall, at the request of the Chairman of the Committee, meet within a period of not more than fifteen days to consider the matter with a view to facilitating a satisfactory solution.

efforts to find a satisfactory solution

---

[1]   It is confirmed that the term "matter" in this paragraph includes any matter which is covered by Multilateral Trade Agreements annexed to the Agreement Establishing the World Trade Organization, in particular those bearing on export and import measures.

Printed in France